Ryan Rebold decide~~d~~ ~~would fulfill his prom~~ ~~ise and at~~ the same time put his faith to the test. Leaving his wife and family behind, he decided to take a seven-day trip alone by Greyhound bus to seven different cities to see how God would take care of him. Would you like to know what happens to Ryan? Would you like to know what God did for him? Then you must read *Nothing But Faith In My Pocket*. This incredible journey of faith will challenge you to do something about your own faith or lack of it. Don't read this book unless you expect to be changed.

—Dr. Elmer Towns
Cofounder, Liberty University
Dean, School of Religion
Award-winning author of *The Names of the Holy Spirit*

"Total surrender—a great statement that all of us desire in our walk with Christ but yet find so difficult to put into practice. Ryan Rebold has given us great insight on what a life totally surrendered to Christ looks like and how we can apply those principles in our own. I strongly recommend *Nothing But Faith In My Pocket* as an important part of your daily journey to know Him and serve Him better."

—Jonathan Falwell
Pastor, Thomas Road Baptist Church
Lynchburg, VA

"I have known Ryan Rebold since he was a little boy. I always had this feeling that God had great plans for his life. When I saw this manuscript, I realized that my premonitions were accurate. You will be challenged and blessed."

—Dr. David Jeremiah
Senior Pastor, Shadow Mountain Community Church
Founder and CEO, Turning Point

NOTHING BUT

FAITH

IN MY

POCKET

NOTHING BUT
FAITH
IN MY
POCKET

a journey off the pew and into the world

W. Ryan Rebold

TATE PUBLISHING
AND ENTERPRISES, LLC

Published by Tate Publishing & Enterprises, LLC
127 E. Trade Center Terrace | Mustang, Oklahoma 73064 USA
1.888.361.9473 | www.tatepublishing.com

Tate Publishing is committed to excellence in the publishing industry. The company reflects the philosophy established by the founders, based on Psalm 68:11,
"The Lord gave the word and great was the company of those who published it."

Book design copyright © 2011 by Tate Publishing, LLC. All rights reserved.
Cover design by Blake Brasor
Interior design by April Marciszewski

Published in the United States of America

ISBN: 978-1-61346-313-0
1. Biography & Autobiography: Personal Memoirs
2. Religion: Christian Life: Spiritual Growth
11.08.15

DEDICATION

To the men of great faith that have changed my life by being an example to me: Dr. Jerry Falwell, Dr. David Jeremiah, Dr. Tim LaHaye, Dr. Tony Foglio, and Dr. Randy Rebold.

> Those who are wise will shine like the brightness of the heavens, and those who lead many to righteousness, like the stars for ever and ever.
>
> Daniel 12:3

ACKNOWLEDGMENTS

To my family, Randy, Gale, Robyn, and Renee: Thank you for being the most amazing family anyone could have had.

To my friends Miguel and Gerard: Thank you for constant iron sharpening and being brothers to me.

To Tate Publishing: Thank you for the opportunity to share my story and to Jaime for your patience and support. Best editor ever!

To the wonderful and talented author Kathie Truitt: Thank you for believing in me and for your help.

To all of the "Letters of Paul" writers: Thank you for your willingness and support that made my adventure what it was—awesome.

To Dr. Chuck Morris, Dr. Tony Foglio, and Dr. Elmer Towns: Thank you for encouragement to write.

To my two sons, Jackson and Parker: I love you and cannot wait for the three of us to go on a faith walk together. Obey Jesus and love others!

To my amazing wife, Shannan: Your love and support gave me the strength to take the first step of faith. I am humbled and blessed to be your husband. SHMILY

TABLE
OF
CONTENTS

Examine yourselves to see whether you are in the faith; test yourselves. Do you not realize that Christ Jesus is in you—unless, of course, you fail the test?

2 Corinthians 13:5

WHERE
IS MY
FAITH?

Why not me? I thought to myself while sitting in the church pew. *Why can't I move a mountain for Christ? Why can't I be used to bring glory to God on a larger scale?* As I sat dwelling on these questions, the answer hit me from the pulpit. "Faith," said the preacher. "Faith will give you wings, or the lack of faith will keep you grounded."

I instantly convinced myself that it wasn't a lack of faith. I knew in my heart that Jesus Christ wasn't only the Son of God and part of the Holy Trinity but that He was also the only one that could pay the debt of sin through His death, burial, and resurrection for mankind. As the preacher spoke about Abraham and what a mighty man of faith he was, I wondered where my own personal faith was. Abraham had the faith to sacrifice his son Isaac out of obedience to God. Yet Abraham also lied and deceived when he was faced with fear, which further encouraged me that, though he was capable of displaying great faith, he too was just human. Though he was called for a specific purpose of being the father of God's people, Abraham still had to put his faith in God.

I thought, *Doesn't faith only have to do with salvation?* Suddenly, as if opening my eyes for the first time to light, I realized I needed to have faith in Christ for every aspect of my life. In my head, I heard, "Do you trust me to take care of what you will eat? Where you will sleep? Though you say you trust me with what will happen to your soul after you die, do you trust me equally as much with the life you are now living?" I wondered if my faith was in Christ or in people and things.

I have never thought of myself as being exceptional in my Christian walk. Actually, the opposite is true. Regretfully, I've had more than my share of times of doing things that did not bring glory to God but to myself. In the late seventies, my father became ordained and a part of the staff of the nationally known Thomas Road Baptist Church, where Dr. Jerry Falwell was the senior pastor. When my sisters, Robyn and Renee, and I were dedicated to the LORD as small children, it was Dr. Falwell that laid hands on me and prayed a prayer of dedication. In the early eighties, my parents then moved our family to El Cajon, California, a suburb of San Diego, where my father became the executive assistant to Dr. David Jeremiah. It was while listening to Dr. Jeremiah on TV one Sunday morning when I was only five years old that I was moved by the Spirit of God to ask my mother how I could become a Christian. There in my home, my mother explained to me the gospel and the death, burial, and resurrection of our LORD, and that day I became a child of the King. A few years later, my father became a part of the Skyline Church in Lemon Grove, California, where Dr.

John Maxwell was the senior pastor. It was while at Skyline I was baptized.

So from early childhood, I knew that I had *saving* faith and that my name was written in the Lamb's Book of Life. From time to time, I would have *serving* faith by participating in church functions and outreach programs, such as helping out at our community events or walking through the neighborhoods handing out information for VBS. But the question that seemed to be in front of me was, did I have *surviving* faith, the faith that would enable me to take on a bear or a lion as young David did? Deep down within me was a desire to have that same kind of boldness. To me, it seemed that Jesus had given clear instruction as to what we as Christians should be called to do. In the book of Matthew, Jesus says:

> Anyone who loves his father or mother more than me is not worthy of me; anyone who loves his son or daughter more than me is not worthy of me; and anyone who does not take his cross and follow me is not worthy of me. Whoever finds his life will lose it, and whoever loses his life for my sake will find it.
>
> Matthew 10:37–39 (NIV)

I thought about the torment that Jesus went through for my sin, and it broke my heart like never before. I knew that Christ dying on the cross was for more than my simply attending church on Sunday and giving ten percent of my paycheck. Though I believed Jesus was my Savior, had I ever allowed Him to be the LORD of my life? This was a hard question for me to come to terms with, since the easiest person in the world to lie to is myself.

Growing up in a Christian home, I never felt that I needed to do more than just play a role in the congregation, like many churchgoers do—much like a spectator. I know there are those Christians that do more than just sit and listen. Sadly, in most of the churches I have visited, many of those were also the same people that made sure everyone knew just how "holy" they were. My heart was heavy and lacked the desire to do more. The more I did, the more of a hypocrite I would be portrayed as.

At that moment, I knew in my heart that I hadn't fully trusted Jesus as LORD of every area of my life. I felt completely unworthy to call myself a Christian. I needed and wanted to get real with God, and I needed and wanted Him to consume my life. If we are truly called to go out into the world and be salt and light, then I was no longer willing to accept the mediocrity I had convinced myself was the normal Christian life. Instead of waiting for a divine burning bush, I—an average husband, father, church member, and businessman—decided to take a step of faith from outside of the pew and with the cross of Jesus, dive into the world.

At first, I wasn't even sure exactly where this new spiritual zealousness was taking me. I had no idea whatsoever what I was going to do. I simply knew I wanted to place myself in a situation in which apart from God and His divine provision I simply could not succeed. I knew in the very core of my being that I wanted my two boys—Jack, three, and Parker, nine months at the time—to one day look at their father and say, "My daddy walked with God." I realized that I couldn't really love my wife as Christ loved the church unless I was willing to walk in the path of Christ and not my own.

Uncertainty and second thoughts began to hit me as doubts regarding my own abilities began to slow my willingness to move forward in obedience. Doubts such as lack of knowledge and fear of failing suffocated me. The more I dwelled on my fears, the more I would need to tell myself to breathe. Fear was holding me in a place of being lukewarm. I remember thinking, *Even if I only consider myself an average church member, God can still use me.* I knew that for me to be used in a mighty way, I would have to do something different and challenging.

The first step of obedience for me was deciding that I would go back to school. Education in my early life hadn't been one of my top priorities. In truth, due to several circumstances at that time in my life, I didn't even finish high school. I did end up completing my GED. From there, I entered into the ministry and family business with my parents, got married, and became a father. Then, at the age of thirty, God seemed to say, "Tag, you're it," and my college career began. I enrolled in online classes with Liberty University Online in Lynchburg, Virginia. The very first class I signed up for was Evangelism 101. I genuinely wanted to learn how to clearly explain to other people what it meant to be a child of God. Though I hadn't had any form of schooling in over thirteen years and was admittedly a little intimidated, I couldn't get enough of that first class. The class was very well designed to simply break down the process of salvation. The first section was about securing my own faith, and then it moved on to some suggested scriptures to share with other people. It started to combat the fear of lack of knowledge. Though I was far from being a theologian or a scholar, I remembered that the disciples were mainly made up of fishermen.

I wanted to go out into the world and leave all that I had in place of comfort. I was inspired to this challenge by looking in the mirror and not seeing much boldness for Christ. I knew that I didn't want to go to a third world country for two main reasons. First, I didn't know any other language. Second, there are plenty that don't know Jesus as LORD and Savior here in the States. Praying for peace about making a change and talking with my wife, I decided to make a plan for a unique trip that wouldn't test God but test my own faith in God. I wanted to be put in situations where my whole life, surroundings, and dependence could only be on God and not what I had formed as a comfort zone. My desire was to do something that would allow me to grow in three main areas of my life: faith in Christ for all things, for Christ to be seen in every area of my life, and boldness to share the gospel with anyone. For me to move a mountain, I would first have to face it.

I grew up with comic books and video games. My generation's idea of a hero was either a Teenage Mutant Ninja Turtle or Superman, played by Christopher Reeves. I have never met anyone who didn't wish that they could fly, be bulletproof, or have superior strength like the man of steel. I'm not a fan of heights and never really thought of flying myself, but I love the ability Superman had to help anyone at any time. However, for me, I think a more realistic hero would have to be Westley, the hero from the movie *The Princess Bride*. When I was nine years old, I was able to see a real hero in action. Here was a man who had no superpowers. He wasn't from some fictional planet in outer space. He was simply a real man.

After losing his love, we find Westley has to fight a skilled swordsman, Inigo Montoya. He defeats him and then meets a giant of a man, literally. Wesley defeats Fezzik, the strong giant, just like his previous enemy. Finally, our hero has to sit face-to-face with the fast-talking, quick-witted mastermind of the villainous gang, named Vizzini. Through a battle of wits, Westley prevails. I remember how I felt as a child when Westley was able to defeat the "best of the best." I felt bold and courageous. I was always the smaller kid that got picked on, but Westley overcame them all. He was courageous, fearless, and victorious. He was able to achieve all of this because he was driven by two things: love and purpose. It was this same kind of drive that I wanted in my life. I wanted to love Christ so much that no obstacle, large or small, could stop me.

My purpose for wanting a God-size adventure like this was not so that people would pat me on the back but to tear down any kind of wall that might exist between God and me. I'm in no way an adrenaline junkie. You would never catch me doing things like bungee jumping or skydiving. I am one of those people who, while sitting on their couch eating junk food and watching challenging game shows like *Wipeout*, says to the TV, "I can do that." In reality, I never really would. Though those shows offer a large cash prize to the winner, money shouldn't be the motivator. The motivation and real reward should come from the doing. It was from these challenging game show settings that I felt that I had a real motivation to do something beyond myself, something that would bring glory to God, and the prize and reward would be in the doing, the obedience. The challenge would be my selfish desires, insecurities, and fears versus God's grace, mercy, will, and love.

Everyday life brings us choices where we can either respond in the Spirit or react in the flesh. Admittedly, it doesn't require a great deal of faith when determining what you will eat when you get in your car, drive to Jack in the Box, and order four tacos, an ultimate cheeseburger on sourdough, and an Oreo milkshake. It doesn't take much faith to know where you will sleep when you walk into your house or apartment and lie down on your bed. For me, these have always been easy things to trust God for. So how was I to step out of my comfort zone? What exactly was God wanting to do in my life? How would I be able to increase my faith? I wondered.

PREPARATION
FOR
REVELATION

The idea quickly developed into a plan. By the conclusion of the service, I had over 95 percent of the plan figured out. Faith beyond my own limits was what drove me to format this idea into action. I determined that the best way for me to be stretched was to leave my wife and children for several days and launch out by myself in a total faith mission. This couldn't just be a trip that would give me the experience of a homeless person. It needed to be larger than that. It doesn't take much faith to talk to a stranger about sports, the weather, or your kids. How about talking to someone about Jesus cold turkey? How about standing and preaching the Word of God? How about not depending on your wallet for food and shelter but on the body of Christ? Combine all three of those different scenarios, and to me, that would be a faith walk.

Though my family and friends know me by my middle name, Ryan, for this trip, I wanted to go by my first name, William. I wanted to be a new me, so even my name would be different. My plan was to travel by Greyhound bus (which I had never done before) to seven different cities during seven consecutive days. Rather than making a list of things I would take with me on my trip like most people do, I developed a list of things that I wouldn't take with me. This list included money and credit cards, a cell phone, or any other form of communication device.

At first I had some anxiety about not having my technological lifelines. I was so used to getting e-mails, text messages, and even the occasional phone call that it had become a part of my life. If I didn't have my phone with me, there was a sense that something was wrong, the feeling like I had left the water running or the stove on.

However, in a way, I was looking forward to this challenge as well. The idea came from Luke chapter ten, where we see Jesus sending out his disciples to do ministry and He instructs them to not take anything for their journey. I did make one major modification to this model, in that I didn't go with someone else to make a pair. On this trip, I was going it alone, humanly speaking.

The first part of my plan involved picking seven major cities that wouldn't be more than four hours apart from one another. Starting in Knoxville, Tennessee, I would head to Chattanooga, Tennessee; Nashville, Tennessee; Louisville, Kentucky; Indianapolis, Indiana; Columbus, Ohio; Cincinnati, Ohio; Lexington, Kentucky; and then back to Knoxville. Next, I determined that I would go to the first Bible-believing church in every city I visited that was in walking distance from the bus station. I would map out ahead of time where the churches would be in order to ensure I didn't walk around the city all day aimlessly looking for one. I wouldn't contact these churches in advance of my coming because I wanted them to respond on the spot. Just as Christ had instructed His disciples in Luke, once I arrived to these churches, I would explain my mission to the church leadership and only ask for housing and food while I was ministering in their city.

After making my initial plans, it was then time for me to sit down with my wife, Shannan, and share with her what I believed God was leading me to do. I needed to present this desire I had in a safe and timely way. I waited until both of our boys went down for their afternoon nap. We sat down in our living room, and I shared how I felt about my lack of faith. It was humbling to confess to my wife that as the leader of our home I needed to grow more.

I started the conversation with just expressing my passion to be bold. When she heard that I wanted to go on a trip with no car, no money, no phone, and only take my ID in case my body was decomposing somewhere, her first reaction was a typical wife's response: "Can you be gone longer than a week?" No, that isn't what she said. Though she was nervous for me, she encouraged me to do whatever I felt I needed to do to have peace with God. She has always been a loving and selfless wife. She expressed that she had never heard of anyone doing anything like this before.

Together, we determined exactly what I would take on my trip: a backpack, a Bible, my driver's license (for ID), a digital camera, business cards to leave with the churches for prayer, a folder with some resources for dealing with other worldviews, seven hundred gospel tracts for evangelism, a poncho with hood in case of bad weather, one change of clothes, and a journal to document my journey as well as for personal growth. Knowing I was going to be away from all of my loved ones and with no way to communicate on a daily basis, I knew I would want to have an encouraging word each day while on my trip, so I decided to ask seven different Christian leaders to write me letters ahead of time, and I would open and read one at the beginning of each day. I would call these letters my "Letters of Paul." Paul wrote so many letters that were encouraging, challenging, and uplifting. I thought that title was appropriate for what I hoped to receive. I asked that each letter include a scripture, an encouraging word, and an action challenge that I would have to do no matter what was asked of me. Since I wanted this trip to take me beyond my limits, I knew that allowing others to challenge me while using their spiritual insight and creativity would help me to surpass my limitations and ideas. The seven people I chose to write my "Letters of Paul" included a dean of biblical studies at a well-known Christian university, three senior pastors, one missionary with an earned doctorate, one associate pastor responsible for writing discipleship programs, and one woman who works with one of the largest women's ministries in the world. Their ages ranged from twenty-eight to sixty-five. Each one was excited for me to take this step of faith. My plan was inspiring to some, while the others expressed the task to be too hard. Whichever side of the fence they were on, each of them encouraged me to step out in faith.

As excited as I was about preparing for my trip, there were some moments of discouragement. I had both family and friends challenge my idea, with some telling me not to go. Some even questioned me about neglecting my responsibilities as a husband and a father. My own father, for whom I have the utmost respect and who has walked with God for many years, didn't want me to go. In those initial days, it seemed at times as if I was already on an island with just me and God. But when confronted with those times of discouragement from others, I was again reminded of the standard that Jesus set in Matthew chapter ten. I couldn't love my wife, kids, or parents more than God. As the leader of my household, I had three major responsibilities: provider, protector, and priest. I couldn't just neglect these, so I needed to talk to my father about them. It was decided that I would take a week of vacation pay so financially my family wouldn't be hindered. My wife was going to be teaching VBS that week, so I felt she was taken care of in that area as well. I asked for fellow brothers in Christ to check in on my wife to make sure she was okay. As most were praying for my safety, I asked them to do the same for my wife and two little boys.

As the date for my departure was approaching, it became time for me to get ready for my trip. I had three months before I wanted to leave. I thought June would be a good time since most young people would be out of school and the weather would be more accommodating. I needed to be physically, mentally, emotionally, and spiritually ready for the journey. When I considered every area I needed to work on, it came down to discipline.

I was going to be walking miles every day with at least a twenty-five-pound pack on my back. In order to be ready physically, I began getting up early in the morning and doing some light jogging in some of the tougher parts of the city. At first, the act of getting up early and jogging wasn't the problem. Being constant with the routine became difficult. I'm not a morning person, and jogging to me is the least enjoyable way to work out. I was never out of shape because I believe "round" is just an expanded shape. I would jog for about fifteen minutes a day for the first week and then add close to ten minutes every week after. It became easier to add more because I viewed it as a challenge. I was able to go for about forty-five minutes with no stops after about a month.

The physical part was coming along much faster than the other areas I needed to prepare for. Mentally, I was doing okay, but I could not really fully adjust to the idea of what my future surroundings could potentially be. At times, my imagination would run wild, and almost every kind of scenario would seem to find its way into my head. I could see myself in the middle of a downtown back alley trying to witness the truth when a pack of rabid dogs came chasing after me. I pictured other believers at the churches I would visit being inspired to come walk with me. I even thought about me being beaten and left for dead with no one knowing where I was at.

Emotionally, I was like a wave in the ocean. There were times when I was excited and could not wait for the test I was about to face, and then moments later I would be fearful of the vast unknown I was about to confront. As far as being ready spiritually, for me it came down to scripture memorization. I needed to chain together a series of scriptures that would enable me to lead someone to the LORD. Dr. Ben Gutierrez, my evangelism professor, wrote a book titled *After Three*. In the book, he gives a great formula for leading somebody to Christ. Using his book as a guide, I decided to memorize the following scriptures:

For all have sinned and fall short of the glory of God.

Romans 3:23 (NIV)

For the wages of sin is death, but the gift of God is eternal life in Christ Jesus our LORD.

Romans 6:23 (NIV)

All of us have become like one who is unclean, and all our righteous acts are like filthy rags.

Isaiah 64:6a (NIV)

He saved us, not because of righteous things we had done, but because of His mercy. He saved us through the washing of rebirth and renewal by the Holy Spirit.

Titus 3:5 (NIV)

For it is by grace you have been saved, through faith and this not from yourselves, it is the gift of God not by works, so that no one can boast.

Ephesians 2:8–9 (NIV)

But God demonstrates his own love for us in this: While we were still sinners, Christ died for us.

Romans 5:8 (NIV)

If you declare with your mouth, "Jesus is LORD," and believe in your heart that God raised him from the dead, you will be saved. For it is with your heart that you believe and are justified, and it is with your mouth that you profess your faith and are saved.

Romans 10:9–10 (NIV)

For, "Everyone who calls on the name of the LORD will be saved."

Romans 10:13 (NIV)

Memorizing and internalizing these Scripture verses was a very important part of my plan. I knew that when I had these scriptures memorized, I would be ready to go. I have a bad case of dyslexia, and memorization doesn't come naturally to me at all. As a child I would get frustrated with reading and therefore didn't put in much effort on reading. I do love music though, and putting Scripture to a rhythm helped me memorize much faster than I thought.

I knew that if anyone was going to come to Christ through this effort, it wouldn't be because of me. I knew that I could not save anyone and it was the Holy Spirit that would change the hardened hearts and bring souls to Christ, not me. In addition to genuinely seeking out those who were lost, I also had a burden to mix it up with those who claimed the name of Christ yet lived so far below their means as a believer. When I met a person who claimed to be a Christian, I wanted them to share their testimony on how they came to have a personal relationship with Christ. If they had never repented of their sins and never turned from their old, worldly ways, I would challenge them to share how they know they were saved. If, on the other hand, they could clearly share with me how they know they were saved, the next thing I would do is encourage those who genuinely were born again to go and talk to someone about Christ like I was doing with them.

With a nonjudgmental mind-set ready to talk to the lost and my fellow believers, I went to GospelTract.org and selected four different gospel tracts to take with me on my journey:

1 Which one of these is right? (pictured eight different religions on the front)

2 The Evolution of Man (picture of a monkey evolving to a grown man then to a man at a computer)

3 Intelligence Test (six fun questions to get people thinking)

4 Are you innocent or guilty? (offered advice for someone's day in court)

My thought was that with this wide variety of tract topics, I would be able leave something with each person after I was able to talk with them.

On June 10, 2009, my father and the rest of the staff in our ministry surrounded me and laid their hands on me and prayed. He was about to leave for a previously scheduled trip and was not going to be available to pray for me on the upcoming Saturday when I was scheduled to leave. As he and the rest of the staff were praying for me, I was also praying and asking God to put a fire into their own hearts in order that they too might be challenged to take a huge step of faith. I knew my father was going to be out of town on the morning I left. At that moment, I remember wishing that he would want to come with me. But even if he had offered, I knew I wouldn't be able to have my father or anyone else go with me. My earthly father would stay behind, but my heavenly Father would be with me. After the prayer time, my father hugged me good-bye, told me he loved me and was proud of me, and left for his trip. I got in my car and went to the downtown Knoxville Greyhound bus station, where I bought the necessary bus pass for my trip.

June 11 had been set aside in order to make a video I titled *See You Later*. It was a home-quality video that I had decided to make to not only document the "event," but I used this tool to record my heartfelt love while at the same time saying good-bye to my wife and two small sons. It was by far one of the most difficult things I have ever had to do. I remember the movie starring Michael Keaton titled *My Life*. In the movie, Keaton's character chose to make videos about his life and lessons he wanted to pass on to his unborn child because he was dying of cancer, and he knew he would not be alive when his child grew up. Remembering that part of the movie is what gave me the idea to say something to my wife and two little boys on camera. Though I truly believed I would return safely from my trip and would more than likely destroy the tape I had made, if for any reason something were to happen to me, at least they would get to see Daddy telling them again that he loved them and encouraging the entire family to be bold for Christ in their lives.

On June 12, I decided to spend the last day before my trip with my family. That day, I was not feeling nervous or even sad. What I do remember feeling was more along the lines of "Let's go and get back already." After spending so much time praying, planning, and preparing for the trip, I was now very anxious to go.

Shannan and I took our boys to Chuck-E-Cheese's for some pizza, their favorite place to go in Knoxville, and we had a great time. My son Jack, though he was only three years old, could beat me at all the car-racing games. Apparently the NASCAR bug infected my son at an early age. After pizza and game playing, the boys and I were dropped off at home, and Shannan went to the store to pick up my travel-size toothpaste. I just wanted to have a few minutes with them to myself. Looking at my sons, thinking about my wife, and knowing I was soon going to have to say good-bye to them made me realize what a blessed life I really do have. Unfortunately, as I pillowed my head for the night, I started to get a bad sore throat, and my left ear was starting to ache.

GOOD MORNING
AND
GOOD-BYE

Saturday, June 13, finally arrived. Waking up with a sore throat made saying good-bye that much more difficult. I grabbed my backpack, kissed Shannan good-bye, and prayed over Jackson and Parker. Though I had gone on a business trip from time to time without them, this was different. No phone calls or video chatting to say goodnight. No comfort of hearing their voices just to hear them. This was nothing like having to say good-bye before.

My good friend and employee Miguel De La Mora took me to the steps of my home church. Meeting us there at four in the morning were the senior and executive pastors of the church, Mark McKeehan and Chuck Morris. My other good friend and employee, Gerard Torrez, met us on the steps of the church via his cell phone because he could not physically be there to pray and lay hands on me before I left. My father surprised me by coming back early from his trip so that he could be there to see me go. With tears of joy, the men prayed for not only my family and me but for those that I would come in contact with on my trip. As each man prayed, I felt more and more ready to go.

After an emotional good-bye from my father, he told me to be safe and shared that he was proud of me. I was honored and humbled to have men of God love me so much that they would take the time to get up that early and do that for me. Miguel then drove me to the bus station. Getting out of his SUV, I said, "If I don't see you here or there, I will see you in the air."

Nervous and excited to start, I sat in the bus station in Knoxville waiting for my bus to come. I was going to ask people two simple questions: *What do you believe, and why?* I decided that if someone made eye contact with me, I would take that as from the LORD and go share my faith with them. I knew that I could manipulate the situation by intentionally avoiding making eye contact with others, but I wanted that to be the sign for me to go talk with them. Unfortunately, that early in the morning, most people didn't even have their eyes open. I believed that God wanted me to stop and breathe in my surroundings, to acknowledge that I was already out of my comfort zone and that I needed to depend on Him, starting now. Finally, my bus arrived; my journey had now officially begun, and I was heading to Chattanooga.

Looking for a seat on the bus, I noticed three young Asian men that were sitting together. There was one open seat by one of the young men, so I decided I would start sharing with them. I took a deep breath and whispered to God, "Here we go!" I asked if the seat was taken, and through a few moments of awkward silence and smiles partnered with looks of confusion, I discovered not one of them spoke English. By this time, the bus was leaving, and the people around me were all asleep, including the young men I was sitting next to. Since everybody else on the bus was asleep, I decided to close my eyes and prayed that my throat would feel better once we arrived in Chattanooga. God definitely granted my body more rest than the actual amount of time I was able to sleep. I had only closed my eyes for about forty minutes, but when I woke up, my ear and throat felt so much better. That little nap helped to restore my strength.

After I got off the bus, I needed to head to the restroom. I know that I am beautifully created in the image of God, but I believe there is a great chance that somewhere in the world a mouse has my bladder and I have its. Knowing this, I intentionally avoided drinking or eating very much of anything, for I didn't want to get stuck in a situation where there were no restroom accommodations. I know as humans, we need to have water to keep from becoming dehydrated, but in my case, even filling the thimble from the Monopoly game with water would create the need for me to go ten minutes later.

While walking into the restroom, I had the map with the directions to the first church I would be contacting in my hand. As I was standing at the urinal, I dropped my map on the restroom floor. It landed in a puddle underneath the urinal where I was at. Now, for men who are familiar with using a public men's room, we know that underneath the porcelain hanging on the wall lie all manner of pure evil. It's just something we guys have come to expect, and we all try very hard not to step in it when using the facilities. It is in this very spot that the map I needed to get me to the church landed. For women, just imagine a puddle of pure evil. Standing there, I couldn't do anything but laugh and say, "Well, I guess the first trial starts now." I was able to salvage my map, and I headed down the street.

While walking to the nearby Seventh Day Adventist Church, the road became narrow, and I noticed that I was walking along a set of train tracks. Trying to find God's divine nature in everything, I was encouraged by the train tracks because they reminded me of God's will. One direction, one way. A train cannot turn unless the track it is on guides it to turn that way. That was exactly what I wanted in my life, the straight and narrow path with Christ alongside me. I needed that goal and a direction that could clearly get me there.

While I was walking for about an hour and beginning to sweat like crazy from the good old humidity of the south, several cars passed me by. Some of the people in the cars smiled, while others gave me a head nod, but no one stopped to see if I needed a ride. I didn't have my thumb out, as I had never hitchhiked with a stranger before, but after an hour of walking, I was ready for a ride. The bus station in Chattanooga was also next to the airport, so I wasn't in an area where there were a lot of people walking. In fact, I was the only one on the street. All of a sudden and from out of nowhere, a green minivan came and pulled up right to me. Through the other side of the window, a large black man smiled and said, "You need a ride?"

I instantly said, "Yes!" Without hesitation, I hopped in the van and thanked God for sending me this transportation. "Thank you so much for the ride."

"No problem. Where you headed?"

I gave him the address to the church and shared with him why I was in Chattanooga and what it was I was doing. "My name is William; what's yours?"

"Jacob."

"Do you attend a church around here?"

"Actually, I attend the Church of God in another city. Just visiting some family down here."

I couldn't help but wonder why he would stop for someone he didn't even know. If it was me, I would have just driven by him without giving him a second thought. "Why did you stop and offer to pick me up?"

He smiled and said, "I just felt like it was what I was supposed to do."

I couldn't believe his answer. I was humbled and so grateful that he cared for a complete stranger so much. I felt humility for realizing that I wouldn't have done the same act of kindness for him. "Thank you for having a caring and serving heart. Dozens of cars drove by, but not one of them stopped." Pausing for a moment, I then said, "I am humbled for the ride. If the situation was reversed, I wouldn't have picked you up."

He looked at me and said, "Just doing unto others is all."

Arriving at the church, I thanked him again for his act of kindness. He wished me well and drove off. Getting to the church two hours earlier than what I had planned enabled me to join the church's Bible school hour. Not being a Seventh Day Adventist myself, I didn't know if that would be an issue or not. Sure enough, it seemed to be an issue with the first person I met. Apparently, the gentleman who welcomed me as I entered the church also taught one of the Bible classes. He asked me, "Where are you from, and what denomination are you?" I sidestepped the second question once he told me that he was a professor at the local Seventh Day Adventist College. I didn't want there to be a wedge between us, whether it be out of tradition or doctrine. Sometimes man-made tradition can separate us from our brotherly love. For the average church member there probably never would have been an issue, but this man had the education that surpasses an average attendee. I shared that I was from Knoxville and just in the city for the day. He introduced me to the senior pastor, and I said to him, "Pastor, I'm only here for the day, and my purpose of being here is share the good news of Christ with the people in your community. I have no place to stay, and I have no food. I was hoping that the church could help me in those two areas."

"I think what you are doing is great, and please be sure to grab some refreshments in the room over there." He smiled and walked away. At this moment I had no place to stay. Since I did not bring bedding with me, I knew I was going to be on the streets unless something changed by the time the services ended.

The gentleman that I first met then invited me to attend his class. The class was a group of all men with an average age of fifty, and me being thirty made me the youngest man in the group. During the class discussion, they talked in general about trying to find a way to meet the needs of people within their community. I spoke up and said, "A buddy of mine told me that when Rick Warren started his church in California, one of the first things he did was to take a census of what the people in the community really needed. Surprisingly, it was potty training. So that is what the church offered." Most of the men nodded their heads in agreement, with the exception of the teacher. I was asked why I was in town. I took a few minutes and shared the reason why I was visiting. When I was done, I noticed the teacher looking right at me with intent.

The teacher once again asked, "What denomination do you follow?"

I thought, *I am not ashamed of what I believe, and if it's an issue, so be it.* "I believe Jesus Christ is the only way to the Father, that apart from Him one cannot be saved from the grip of sin. If we can have common ground on that, does it really matter what denomination any of us are with?" I did not want to come across as rude; I just did not want to put a wedge between me and the body of Christ. I often wonder if Jesus was walking the earth today, what answer would He give?

An older gentleman named Billy Campbell looked at me and said, "Amen! That is what matters, not what day you attend church." I immediately liked Billy. At the end of the class, Billy took me to the room where they had their welcome food. Billy was an older man in his late sixties, and he introduced me to his foster son, Naz. He shared that he and his wife were going through the potty-training process with Naz, who was two years old.

I smiled and said, "My son Jackson just accomplished that very thing two days ago." We laughed together as we compared and shared the war stories of the whole potty-training experience.

I then attended the worship service, where they rocked. The message was about Simon, who carried the cross for Jesus when He could no longer do so on His walk to Calvary. It was a timely message for me, as I was thinking about wanting to carry my own cross for Christ. Sitting in the service by myself, I meditated on the scripture that was being shared. It echoed my desire to serve and surrender fully to Christ.

At the end of the service, Billy was talking with another gentleman from the class, whose name is Brath. Brath offered to give me a ride into town, where he knew there would be a lot of people to talk to. He was already giving another man named Darrell a ride and had room for one more. The senior pastor, though offering me zero help, patted me on the back as I walked out the door. At that moment, I realized that this first church would not be helping me with my physical needs, at least not through the church leadership.

While saying good-bye to another man that had been in the Bible class group, Billy called me over. He looked me in the eye and said, "Be safe." While shaking my hand, he slipped me a twenty-dollar bill. I had never asked anyone there for money, but Billy had the reflection of God on his heart. He demonstrated to me that he was a man of faith and that he definitely walked with God. He gave me his e-mail address and wanted me to e-mail him about my trip once I got back. After thanking Billy for his generous gift, I hopped in the truck with Brath and Darrell and headed into the city.

FEAR
LEADS TO
FAILURE

Brath pulled into a little strip mall. He and Darrell then prayed with me, and afterward I thanked them for the ride and headed down the sidewalk. Brath had dropped me off in a highly populated area. However, it was a predominantly Hispanic community. The first ten people I came to didn't speak English. Even though I didn't speak Spanish, I still attempted to talk to people in the area. Starting to get frustrated around 2:30 p.m., I noticed a man sitting and waiting for the city bus. As I was walking to him, I could see that he had some needs. He was a young man in his early twenties. He had on sweatpants and a white t-shirt with holes in it. He was the first Caucasian I had seen since Brath dropped me off. When I was about eight feet away, I introduced myself.

"Hello, sir, my name is William. What is your name?"

"Ben," he said with a soft, cracked voice. He was definitely shy but seemed to be lonely. Not making much eye contact, I continued talking with him.

"Ben, do you have a few minutes that I can ask you some questions?" I could tell by now that Ben had some slight form of Down syndrome because of his lack of concentration and attentiveness.

"Yes."

"Ben, what do you believe happens to us after we die?"

"Well, I am going to heaven." At first his answer was what any Christian would want to hear, but I needed to know more. Though he answered my question, his attention still seemed to be away from me.

"Why do you believe you will go to heaven?"

He looked up at me and said, "Because I have Jesus in my heart."

There are several people who claim to be Christians, believing that Jesus is in their heart. However, they have never repented of their sins, and their lives don't bear any fruit. I went over every point with Ben to make sure Christ was truly in his life. He confirmed that it meant the same to him as well. I gave him one of my tracts and encouraged him to pass it along to someone else. He took it and gave the first smile I had received all afternoon.

I turned down the street and sat on a patch of grass. At this point, I decided to read one of my first "Letters of Paul." All the letters from those who had written them at my request were put in white envelopes. I did not know which one was from whom. As the LORD would have it, the first letter was from my senior pastor, Mark McKeehan. He wrote:

> Dear Ryan,
>
> Grace, mercy, peace, and comfort to you, my brother. I do not know on which day you will read my letter, but I want you to know I am

praying for you. I am proud of you and for this journey you are on. There is no doubt that you are and will continue to grow because of this faith walk. You are no doubt tired, hungry, and dirty. I am praying Ephesians 6:10–20 for you:

> Finally, be strong in the LORD and in his mighty power. Put on the full armor of God, so that you can take your stand against the devil's schemes. For our struggle is not against flesh and blood, but against the rulers, against the authorities, against the powers of this dark world and against the spiritual forces of evil in the heavenly realms. Therefore put on the full armor of God, so that when the day of evil comes, you may be able to stand your ground, and after you have done everything, to stand. Stand firm then, with the belt of truth buckled around your waist, with the breastplate of righteousness in place, and with your feet fitted with the readiness that comes from the gospel of peace. In addition to all this, take up the shield of faith, with which you can extinguish all the flaming arrows of the evil one. Take the helmet of salvation and the sword of the Spirit, which is the word of God.
> And pray in the Spirit on all occasions with all kinds of prayers and requests.

With this in mind, be alert and always keep on praying for all the LORD's people. Pray also for me, that whenever I speak, words may be given me so that I will fearlessly make known the mystery of the gospel, for which I am an ambassador in chains. Pray that I may declare it fearlessly, as I should.

Ephesians 6:10–20 (NIV)

Ryan, keep on the armor and stay close to the LORD. No matter what comes at you today...God is bigger. My thought for you today is how big is God? Before you answer, let me clarify... I'm not asking how big you think he is but how big are you living him out. I have been living with a passage from 2 Samuel 23 for a while. Today I want you to read it and think about this... what if your biggest opportunity today is wrapped up in your greatest risk or biggest fear? Read 2 Samuel 23:20–23.

Benaiah son of Jehoiada, a valiant fighter from Kabzeel, performed great exploits. He struck down Moab's two mightiest warriors. He also went down into a pit on a snowy day and killed a lion. And he struck down a huge Egyptian. Although the Egyptian had a spear in his hand, Benaiah went against him with a club. He snatched the spear from the Egyptian's hand and killed him with his own spear. Such were the exploits of Benaiah son of Jehoiada; he too was as famous as the three mighty warriors. He was held in greater honor than any of the Thirty, but he was not included among the Three. And David put him in charge of his bodyguard.

2 Samuel 23:20–23 (NIV)

How big is God? A small god can be the cause of a hundred lesser evils. A big God can provide the solution to ten thousand temporal problems! Below I have added some thoughts from a book I had read called *In a Pit with a Lion on a Snowy Day*. I hope you enjoy! Today I want to challenge you to become a lion chaser and to live as though God is bigger than anything coming at you today. It is also the difference between scaredy-cats and lion chasers! If your god is smaller than a 500-pound lion, you'll run away! But if your God is bigger than a 500-pound lion, you might just muster the moral courage to chase lions!

Let me state the obvious: Benaiah was not the odds-on favorite in any of these encounters. He was doubled-teamed by two mighty Moabites. He had to be a two-to-one underdog. If I'm placing bets on an average-size Israelite with a club or a giant Egyptian with a spear, I'm going to put my money on the sharp, pointy thing! And I don't even know how you begin to calculate the odds of man vs. lion. Not only do fully grown lions weigh up to 500 pounds and run 35 mph, their vision is five times better than a human with 20/20 vision. This lion had a huge advantage in a dimly lit pit. And I guarantee that a sure-footed lion with catlike reflexes certainly gains the upper paw in snowy, slippery conditions. Doesn't it seem like Benaiah is choosing his battles poorly? He's outmanned and outsized! And this guy goes on to become commander in chief of Israel's army.

Most of us don't like being in pits with lions on snowy days, but those are the stories worth telling. Those are the experiences that make life worth living! So lion chasers don't try to avoid situations where the odds are against them. Lion chasers know that impossible odds set the stage for amazing miracles!

And here's the rest of the story. Finding yourself in a pit with a lion on a snowy day seems to qualify as bad luck or a bad day. But stop and think about it. Can't you just see David flipping through résumés looking for a bodyguard? I majored in security at Jerusalem U. Nope. I did an internship with the Temple guard. Don't call us; we'll call you. I worked for Brinks Armored Chariots. Thanks but no thanks. Then he comes to Benaiah's résumé: *I killed a lion in a pit on a snowy day.* You've got to admit, that looks awfully good on your résumé if you're applying for a bodyguard position with the king of Israel. What seemed like a bad break turned into a big break, and those impossible odds set the stage for his entire military career! I think there is part of us that wants God to reduce the odds. We like situations where the odds are in our favor. But sometimes God allows the odds to be stacked against you so He can reveal more of His glory!

It is so easy to read about a lion encounter that happened three thousand years ago and totally underestimate the fear factor. Sure, he killed the lion. But not before it scared the living daylights out of him. He was inches from thirty bared teeth. I don't think he ever forgot the smell of the lion's bloody breath. And the sound of the roar had to echo in his mind's ear forever! I don't care how battle-tested or battle-scarred you are. I don't care how crazy or courageous you are. You don't come face-to-face with a 500-pound lion without experiencing sheer terror or pure fear! But one thing sets lion chasers apart. *They don't run away from the things that scare them!*

Normal people don't chase lions, but lion chasers aren't normal. I mean honestly, the natural reaction is to run away! The greatest experiences will often double as the scariest experiences. The defining moments will often double as the scariest decisions. Imagine the bedtime stories Benaiah must have told his children! I can hear his kids: *Tell us the lion story one more time!* I think we owe it to our kids and grandkids to live our lives in a way that is worth telling stories about. And more importantly, we owe it to God.

So here is my question: *are you living your life in a way that is worth telling stories about?* Maybe it is time to quit running and start chasing. The people God uses the most are often the people who have experienced the most adversity. I think all three encounters recorded in 2 Samuel 23—taking on two Moabite warriors, a giant Egyptian, and a 500-pound lion—could have ended Benaiah's military career! If you're dead, your career is generally over with! They were *make or break* moments!

On one level this seems like a mistake, but what if Benaiah and a buddy had defeated a single Moabite? Or what if Benaiah had defeated a small Egyptian? Or chased his cat into a pit on a sunny day and found it? I'm pretty sure we wouldn't be reading about it. But without those adverse conditions, Benaiah would have disappeared from the pages of Scripture! It was adversity that turned into an opportunity for Benaiah to prove himself as a valiant warrior.

God is in the remodeling business. And He cares more about your long-term potential than your short-term comfort. If you let Him, He'll turn past adversities into future opportunities! You don't have to go looking for adversity. It will find you. And when it does, don't run away! If you have the courage to chase the lion into the pit on a snowy day, you may just discover your destiny in the middle of that adversity!

I know one thing for sure: none of these encounters were planned. Benaiah didn't wake up on the morning of his lion encounter and plan out every detail. It wasn't scheduled in *Outlook*. It wasn't on his *to-do* list. I'm not even sure it was on his *wish list*. We tend to read the Bible as a textbook instead of a storybook. Killing the lion in real time was not a foregone conclusion! Hand-to-hand combat with another human is one thing. Humans have tendencies. You can predict punches and counterpunches with a higher level of certainty. But savage beasts tend to be volatile and unpredictable. Their actions and reactions are less certain. This could have gone either way! But remember that God will call you to places and to do things that will require total reliance on him! When you follow Christ, you never know where you may end up! I am living proof of that. You have to jump in; do not wait for the perfect time, the perfect condition. If Benaiah had waited for the perfect condition, he would have never killed the lion or done any other things that he did.

Most of the good things that have happened are the byproducts of risk! There is an old saying that says opportunity knocks. *Opportunity doesn't knock.* The giant Egyptian that Benaiah did battle with didn't knock *on* the door. He knocked *down* the door. Most of us want our opportunities gift wrapped. We want our lions stuffed or caged or cooked medium well and served on a silver platter. But opportunities typically present themselves at the most inopportune time in the most inopportune place. Opportunities often come disguised as big, hairy, audacious problems, but lion chasers don't see problems. They see 500-pound opportunities!

How do I see them? Prayer! People who pray see opportunities that others, who do not pray, never even see because they are opportunity blind! One of our greatest spiritual shortcomings is low expectations. We don't expect much from God because we aren't asking for much. When my prayer life is hitting on all eight cylinders, I can believe God for everything. But when I'm in a prayer slump, I have a hard time believing God for anything. Low expectations are the byproduct of prayerlessness, but prayer has a way of God-sizing our expectations. The more you pray, the higher your expectations!

When Benaiah saw the lion, he didn't see a problem but an opportunity! Deep down inside, I think all of us have this primal longing to do something crazy for God. We want to build an ark or kill a giant or chase a lion. We want to do something great for God. That is why you are where you are today.

Here's a lion chaser's manifesto. Quit living as if the purpose of life is to arrive safely at death. Grab life by the mane. Set God-sized goals. Pursue God-ordained passions. Go after a dream that is destined to fail without divine intervention. Keep asking questions. Keep making mistakes. Keep seeking God. Stop pointing out problems and become part of the solution. Stop repeating the past and start creating the future. Stop playing it safe and start taking risks. Expand your horizons. Accumulate experiences. Consider the lilies. Enjoy the journey. Find every excuse you can to celebrate everything you can. Live like today is the first day and last day of your life. Don't let what's wrong with you keep you from worshiping what's right with God. Burn sinful bridges. Blaze a new trail. Criticize by creating. Worry less about what people think and more about what God thinks. Don't try to be who you're not. Be yourself. Laugh at yourself. Quit holding out. Quit holding back. Quit running away.

Ryan, here is my big challenge for you today…here is your lion to chase today! Do whatever it takes to make money today. Sing on the corner of the street, do a skit, beg, whatever you have to do besides compromising and sinning... do it! Then take the money and buy you and a homeless friend a hot meal. This will allow you to be Jesus even more for someone who may need Jesus and is probably hungrier than you. Remember what Jesus said in Matthew 25:

> I was a stranger and you did not invite me in, I needed clothes and you did not clothe me, I was sick and in prison and you did not look after me. They also will answer, "LORD, when did we see you hungry or thirsty or a stranger or needing clothes or sick or in prison, and did not help you?" He will reply, "Truly I tell you, whatever you did not do for one of the least of these, you did not do for me."
>
> Matthew 25:43–45 (NIV)

I am proud of you, and I am praying for you and for your family at home. I cannot wait to hear about it when you arrive.

To God be the Glory and His grace be upon you each day of your journey,

Mark

Pastor Mark's letter really encouraged me. I felt pumped, and at that moment, I needed the encouragement since the church hadn't come through as I had hoped. I looked for opportunities in order to reach the challenge that Pastor Mark had set for me. I looked for a homeless person that

I could bless with a meal. There were none to be found in the area that I was at, so I went back to witnessing, keeping in mind what challenge was before me.

After trying to witness for several hours, the reality began to hit me that I didn't have a place to stay. Knowing that I had no place to stay in a city that hadn't been open to my sharing the gospel, I found myself free falling into complete fear.

Walking up to a closed Baptist church, I began to cry. At thirty years old, I fell on my knees and wept my eyes out to God. I felt abandoned and alone. Even after pleading with Him to send comfort and help, I didn't get anything. No answer at all. Why had the church not helped me, even though Billy and Brath had?

At that moment, in my mind I wiped the dust from my feet and decided to quit. Not feeling prepared enough to take this trip on without the help of others, I chose to quit and take the last bus back to Knoxville. I convinced myself that I would just try another time when God was a little more "willing" to help me.

Walking back to the bus stop, I noticed the train track that ran behind it. I decided to avoid people and just walk along the track. Engulfed with self-pity and fear, I didn't notice the train that was coming behind me. A simple gust of wind caused me to turn my head halfway, and there, less than a hundred yards from me, was the train engine coming right at me. It seemed that everything slowed down around me at that moment. Instinctively, I quickly jumped down a small hill to avoid the train, and in doing so, I twisted my right knee. Once the train had passed, I grabbed my bag that had slid farther down the hill and started to hobble toward the bus stop.

Now that my knee was beginning to swell up, it was taking me longer to get back to the station. By the time I arrived there, I had just missed the last bus back to Knoxville by ten minutes. I would have made it in plenty of time had I not gotten hurt. Now what was I going to do?

I remembered what that same train track had meant to me earlier that day. To be in God's will, I need to go in His direction and not my own. If we try to do things our way, God may send a train to stop us. Now I would have to wait for four hours before I could get a ride into Nashville. I knew by the time I would get there, I would not be able to talk to the church I had mapped because it would then be after ten o'clock in the evening.

I noticed that there were only two other people in the bus station with me. One was a young lady that worked there and was sitting behind the counter; the other was a man evidently waiting for a bus like I was.

"Do you need anything?" the young woman asked me. She was a Caucasian with black hair and slightly overweight. She seemed like a very sociable person.

"No, I am fine, thank you," I said quietly.

"Are you sure? Your knee doesn't look too good. Would you like some ice?" she asked with concern in her voice.

"Yes, please. That would be great." I felt compassion and genuine concern, and it made me smile. I thought, *Why can't more people be like her?* She introduced herself; her name was Daphnie.

While she went to the back of the building to get the ice, the man who was there came up to me and asked, "Do you need some?" He was about six feet tall, black, and couldn't weigh more than a hundred pounds.

I could tell he was offering to provide me with drugs. "No, thank you. I don't touch that stuff." He shared that his name was Timothy.

"How did you hurt your knee?"

"I fell down a rock hill jumping out of the way of an oncoming train. I took it as a shortcut trying to catch the next bus home." I explained to him why I was in the city and why I was leaving.

He said something that surprised me: "God will not give you more than you can handle." I was numb. I didn't know how to respond to him. He got up and walked away.

Upon her return with the ice, Daphnie shared with me that she was a Christian and that her favorite website was one that had been created for homosexual Christians.

She explained that she knew in Leviticus God had said homosexuality was wrong, but she went on to explain that she and Jesus had an arrangement. "I know who I am, and I know who Jesus is to me," she said proudly.

I said, "God is not the author of confusion. How then can He say it is okay for you but not okay for someone else?" She did not respond. Though it was only a few seconds of uncomfortable silence, I could see from her face that she was still trying to find a way to justify her belief. I continued with, "The second commandment talks about idolatry. It seems you have taken the truths of Christ and conformed them to fit what you want instead of what He wants. I don't think you are an evil person or that God doesn't love you. I encourage you to look at your life and let the Word of God be the filter for it."

She smiled. "Thank you for not condemning me to hell. I get that a lot."

"I do not control who goes to heaven and who goes to hell. It really doesn't matter what you or I think but what He says."

She encouraged me to continue on my trip and reminded me that I shouldn't try to see all that God has for me before it happens. She added, "Be careful in the Nashville bus station. The crime there is so bad that it is one of the most dangerous stations in the South." I felt encouraged but a little unsettled about going to Nashville. I was praying the church there would receive me much better than the one in Chattanooga.

On her own, she treated me to lunch. I didn't ask her for anything, and here I was getting more help from her than I had from the leadership of a church. God brought a homosexual and a drug dealer to minister to me when I felt defeated. Just an hour earlier I had asked Him for help and didn't feel that He was going to send any. I was now humbled and humiliated, for here I was trying to come into the city and show others the love of Christ and share His promise of salvation and I was the one being ministered to.

I decided to break one of my trip's own cardinal rules and get a hold of Miguel back in Knoxville by phone. I wanted him to meet me at the bus station in Knoxville with crutches and an Ace bandage. I would continue on from there. In order for me to get back to Knoxville from Chattanooga, I had to first take the last bus to Nashville. Once there, I would then take a bus to Knoxville. I thanked both Daphnie and Timothy for their kind words and prayed with them before leaving. I decided to open my eyes to what God had planned for me and not what I thought I wanted.

On the bus trip to Nashville, I sat by Annette, an older woman who was heading home herself. She shared that she had come to Christ two weeks before and that she had been an alcoholic her entire adult life. I started to see that most people were willing to open up and share their life stories if I first showed them I cared enough to sit and listen. It had been two weeks since she had a drink, and she was really excited for where her life was going.

"That is so great. I am very proud of you!" I said.

Then the mood changed dramatically. She sadly put her head down and then looked up again at me. "My children don't respect me, and one of my kids mistreats me." With tears forming in her eyes, she asked, "What can I do?" I could tell that this was a huge pain in her life and that she really was hurting. The first tear came down, and her voice cracked a little as she finished talking. While her lip slightly quivered, I spoke from my heart.

"Forgive them," I said. "Two weeks ago, you surrendered your life to Jesus, and in doing so, you confessed all of your sins to Him, and He forgave you instantly. We are called to forgive as He forgives. You have to give them time to see the change you have made in your life. How they choose to respond to who you are now is between them and God. Love them. Forgive them. Focus on your heart and cling to Christ."

Tears rolling down her face, she smiled and said, "Thank you. I am glad you were on this bus."

At that very moment, the Spirit of God convicted my heart, and I thought to myself, *I wasn't supposed to even be here, according to my plan.* But I was there now, and I was so grateful I was able to help encourage an older woman who was my younger sister in Christ.

After we arrived in Nashville, I quickly boarded the bus to Knoxville. It was now after 1:00 a.m., and everyone was asleep, so I chose to shut my eyes as well. When I arrived in Knoxville around 5:15 a.m., Miguel was waiting for me, and I felt ashamed to be there. I shouldn't have gone back. I didn't even go twenty-four hours without having to see someone I knew. He gave me some Aleve, a set of crutches, and an Ace bandage. He then encouraged me to keep going. I thanked him and told him, "I am in it for good now." God wouldn't have to send any more trains my way.

I took him back to his place and drove myself back to the bus station. I was having a hard time with the crutches and had a few hours before my bus was scheduled to leave to see if I could handle it or not. The Greyhound pass I had purchased allowed me to ride wherever I wanted to go for seven consecutive days as long as there was a seat available on the bus. Unfortunately, the next bus to Nashville that would have gotten me there before noon was full, and I and one other passenger would have to wait for the next bus, not leaving until that evening. In my mind, I again began calculating. I knew this wouldn't work since I would again be getting in so late that I would miss getting to go to the church and thus wouldn't even have an opportunity to ask them for assistance.

The other passenger waiting with me was a girl from Aruba, and she couldn't afford to miss her bus, as her friends were waiting for her in Nashville so they could fly back together. She told me her name was Areliss. She was a huge Dolly Parton fan and had gone to Pigeon Forge, Tennessee, the day before to attend the Dollywood parade, where Dolly Parton would be in person. I remembered the challenge that Pastor Mark had given me, and I asked her if she would give me five dollars to buy a homeless man outside a meal. I said

I would sing for her when I came back. I was nervous to sing since I am more of a back row choir member than a soloist.

When I walked outside of the bus terminal, I noticed a skinny black man across the street. Given the dirt all over him and a bag next to him, it appeared that he had been on the streets for some time. As I approached him I could see underneath his worn down red hat he had several gray hairs coming out the sides. When I asked him if I could get him something to eat, his face lit up as if I just told him he won the lottery. I had a great time ministering with Charlie. He ate, I spoke, and then we prayed. He just wanted something out of the vending machine, so our time was quick. He was hoping to make some money doing some odd jobs and needed to get to his corner. He thanked me, and I went back inside.

I offered to get my car and drive Areliss to the airport. Reluctantly she said okay. She took a picture of my license and sent it to her friend in case she never made to the airport. Going to the airport, I found out she did not have enough money for the flight, so I borrowed her phone and called my friend Gerard. I explained to him her situation as well as mine. He said to drive to our office and leave my car there and that he would then drive us both to Nashville. I was honored to have friends that would drop everything to help me get back on track.

Gerard, his eleven-month-old son Malachi, Areliss, and I loaded up in the car and headed out. We stopped in Cookeville, Tennessee, to get some Jack in the Box fast food. Areliss had never eaten there, and out of all of the fast food restaurants available today, Jack in the Box is by far my favorite. I explained that I would get two of the world's best tacos for ninety-nine cents. We bought her some tacos, and she loved them.

During the three-hour trip to Nashville, Gerard and I both shared the love of Jesus with her. We arrived at the Nashville airport and got her to her friends earlier than she would have if she had taken the bus or a plane. Next, Gerard dropped me off at the church, and he kept the crutches with him and drove back to Knoxville. I decided that I was going to walk with my bad leg as it was. When I thought about the suffering that Christ went through while carrying a cross that was meant for me, I realized my leg was nothing to hinder me from walking on. Again, the LORD had provided in a way totally unexpected but greatly appreciated.

HUMBLED
AND
DETERMINED

By the time I arrived at the church, the morning service was already letting out, and the pastoral staff was unavailable. The person that was available was a full-time school bus driver who also filled the role as pastor for the small Japanese congregation that met in the same church building later that day. Pastor Barry invited me to come back to the church later that afternoon and attend their service. At this point I did not have assistance from the church; however, I was looking forward to hearing the Word shared for encouragement. It was just about noon, so I took a deep breath with my eyes closed and thanked God for allowing me a new day. Since I had a few hours before the service, I headed excitedly down the street because of the sight that was before me. The day before, I had had few opportunities to share my faith. On this day, however, there was an ocean of people within my reach.

As the LORD would have it, it just so happened to be the last day of the Country Music Festival, and it was estimated that there were close to 80,000 people within a ten-block radius. Before I jumped into evangelizing, I sat down to read another one of my "Letters of Paul." As I did, I remembered that I hadn't sung to Areliss as I had been challenged to do in my first letter, so I knew I would have to complete that challenge sometime before my trip was completed.

My second "Letter of Paul" was written by Jamie Thompson. Jamie is not only a longtime family friend, but she is also the associate director of events for Angel Ministries under the leadership of Dr. Bill Graham's daughter, Anne Graham Lotz. Jamie's letter said:

> Ryan,
>
> God laid you on my heart last night, and so I am the one who's decided to write you this letter. I've prayed through Psalm 31 for you (and will include it for you at the bottom to read from The Message), but I have a strong sense from the LORD that you will read this particular passage for a particular reason *today*.
>
> I'm not sure where you are in your week-long faith walk, but I trust each day will be filled with its great challenges as well as extreme joys as all of your senses are engaged in serving God like never before. You are desperate for Him. Listening to Him. Waiting on Him to whisper the simplest instruction. You are dependent upon Him for food, for a roof over your head (or maybe just stars), for kindness from strangers, and for emotional,

mental, physical, and spiritual stamina. I gather that, by now, you are already praising God for allowing you this opportunity, for you will never be the same.

You will see life differently. You will view the ministry of churches differently. You will regard a simple piece of bread differently. You will observe God's Word and the importance of alone time differently. You will appreciate your family and the comforts of your own home differently. You will be different, and, because *you* are different, all of those around you will be different too. Maybe not right away, but just watch and pray and see how God moves through your simple willingness to be obedient.

I read a quote the other day that reads, "Obedience is the way we show God we love him, and obedience must always come before understanding." Do you understand a new attribute of God even now because of your obedience? Are you viewing lost souls in a different light because of your obedience? Do you understand the depths of man's depravity, perhaps even a sin area of your own life differently because of your obedience? Praise God that He calls us, and when we are obedient, it is because He wants to take us to places with Him in this life that we'd never seek out on our own—usually because they are hard roads, but as you will soon reconfirm, so, so worth it! I am praying for you, Ryan, even now as I write this letter and am asking God to "open the eyes of your understanding" so that you might know the riches of walking with Christ.

That being said, here is my challenge, or task, for you today … John 15:16 says, "You did not choose me, but I chose you and appointed you so that you might go and bear fruit—fruit that will last—and so that whatever you ask in my name the Father will give you." With the truth in mind that God has already appointed you to specific fruit-bearing tasks today, I challenge you to boldly ask in Jesus's name for the opportunity to cross paths with a home-less person. After doing homeless ministry for a few years in college, I observed that they are the ones with the most free time, the most unique stories, and some of the most mixed-up views of God and religion. Help a man, woman, or teenager along in their spiritual journey by taking the time (however long it takes) to truly hear them out, to really dem-onstrate that you love them because they are a child of God, and to share the good news of Jesus with them—all the while boldly asking God for their salvation.

Not knowing the demographics of the cit-ies you're in, if you do not cross paths with a homeless person, my challenge is to use your five senses to show the love of Christ to individuals today: sound—tell someone about Jesus; sight—take a picture with your camera that, to you, captures a moment of Jesus making Himself known to the world whether people are aware of it or not; touch—does someone around you need a squeeze on the shoulder, a pat on the back and a smile, a handshake when others might be keeping their distance because they smell or are dirty? Sometimes we truly are the hands and feet of Christ; taste—did someone provide food for you today that God would have you give away to someone else who might be even hungrier than you are at this moment?; smell—are the smells of the street almost too much to bear? Are your own smells making you insecure and ashamed to share your faith and yet you need to push through? If you've gone hungry for some time, use the smells around you that are so enticing to spur you on today to pray for countries around the world whose people are going hungry along with you—pray that they come to know Jesus as their bread of life!

I will be praying for this challenge and look forward to hearing what God does! So, my friend, I will leave you with the scripture mentioned above that I prayed over you. Be honest with God. Are you feeling any of these same emotions that David felt? Are you in need of God to show up in some of the same areas? If so, claim it! God's Word is for *you*!

I run to you, God; I run for dear life.

Don't let me down!
Take me seriously this time!
Get down on my level and listen,
and please—no procrastination!
Your granite cave a hiding place,
your high cliff aerie a place of safety.

You're my cave to hide in,
my cliff to climb.
Be my safe leader,
be my true mountain guide.
Free me from hidden traps;
I want to hide in you.
I've put my life in your hands.
You won't drop me,
you'll never let me down.

I hate all this silly religion,
but you, God, I trust.
I'm leaping and singing in the circle of
     your love;
you saw my pain,
you disarmed my tormentors,
You didn't leave me in their clutches
but gave me room to breathe.
Be kind to me, God—
I'm in deep, deep trouble again.
I've cried my eyes out;
I feel hollow inside.
My life leaks away, groan by groan;

my years fade out in sighs.
My troubles have worn me out,
turned my bones to powder.
To my enemies I'm a monster;
I'm ridiculed by the neighbors.
My friends are horrified;
they cross the street to avoid me.
They want to blot me from memory,
forget me like a corpse in a grave,
discard me like a broken dish in the trash.
The street-talk gossip has me
"criminally insane"!
Behind locked doors they plot
how to ruin me for good.

Desperate, I throw myself on you:
you are my God!
Hour by hour I place my days in your
     hand,
safe from the hands out to get me.
Warm me, your servant, with a smile;
save me because you love me.
Don't embarrass me by not showing up;
I've given you plenty of notice.
Embarrass the wicked, stand them up,
leave them stupidly shaking their heads
as they drift down to hell.
Gag those loudmouthed liars
who heckle me, your follower,
with jeers and catcalls.

What a stack of blessing you have piled up
for those who worship you,
Ready and waiting for all who run to you
to escape an unkind world.
You hide them safely away
from the opposition.
As you slam the door on those
oily, mocking faces,
you silence the poisonous gossip.
Blessed God!
His love is the wonder of the world.
Trapped by a siege, I panicked.
"Out of sight, out of mind," I said.
But you heard me say it,
you heard and listened.

Love God, all you saints;
God takes care of all who stay close to him,
But he pays back in full
those arrogant enough to go it alone.

Be brave. Be strong. Don't give up.
Expect God to get here soon.

Psalm 31 (MSG)

May God lead, protect, and keep you!

Blessings,

Jamie Thompson

Whenever the situation presented itself, I would perform the challenge that Pastor Mark had set for me, but the challenge presented by Jamie went to the forefront of my mind immediately. Reading Jamie's letter gave me lighter feet to move with. I didn't have the same fear and concern as I did the day before. Her questions made me face the current state of my emotions. I wanted God so desperately to show up the day before and felt as David did. I really started to sense my faith being stretched and was excited to get moving again.

Walking down the street, I noticed a man sitting down by himself. He was wearing a dark baseball cap but without any design on it. He had a long brown beard that almost covered his entire mouth. I didn't know if he was homeless or just taking a break from walking. I asked him if I could sit down next to him. He responded with a head nod but with no eye contact.

From the outset of the conversation, I could tell that this man was not completely in touch with reality. He did not seem focused or in touch with all that was going on around him or even with me right beside him. Our conversation was different than any other that I had ever had.

His name was Bruce, and no matter what I asked him, his answer was yes to every question.

"Do you believe in Jesus Christ as LORD and Savior?"

"Yes."

"Do you believe you are Jesus Christ?"

"Yes."

"Do you believe I am Jesus Christ?"

"Yes."

So on and on it went. Because I knew that Bruce would say yes no matter what I asked, I decided to ask him if I could pray with him. He naturally said yes, so as we prayed, I asked God to give Bruce clarity in order that he might know God's will clearly in his life. After thanking and saying good-bye to Bruce, I got up and began walking toward the 80,000-plus army of people that was gathered before me. Though my conversation with Bruce wasn't as long as I was hoping it would be, I did feel the reason for that divine appointment was as a direct result of what Jamie had asked me to do. From that point on I would look for opportunities to spend more time with the homeless as opposed to being solely focused on presenting the gospel.

As I walked around looking at all of the different venues available to the public, I had the opportunity to talk to a lot of different people. Not being a huge country music fan myself, I definitely felt out of my comfort zone. I tried to bring God or Jesus into each conversation as soon as possible. Most conversations ended quickly if they were not first about the weather, the festival, or who their favorite artist was. Unfortunately, when they would in turn ask me who my favorite artist was, I would say Chris Rice or Jimmy Needham. Neither are country musicians, and they would just walk away from there. Bruce was the only homeless person that I came into contact with, and my comfort zone was thwarted with the surroundings of cowboys and cowgirls. I was able to plant many seeds, but not one person had received Christ yet.

I looked at my watch and determined it was time I headed back to the church. From the time I had left home, it had been two days, three buses, one van ride, several miles hobbling in hot, humid weather, and *no shower*. I was beyond simply smelling bad; I stunk. I was that guy. You know the one I am talking about, the one you will walk completely out of the way to avoid because of the nasty scent he gives off. If you don't know what I am talking about, perhaps you should go take a shower and see if more people come around your way. Knowing I was carrying an offensive odor, I wanted to be as far away from people as I could but without being rude at the same time.

Walking into the church, I noticed a small group of about fifteen people meeting together in one of the classrooms. Having never been in a Japanese/English-speaking service before, I was excited to hear the word of God being shared with these people regardless if I could understand what was being said. The pastor would switch from one language to the other all throughout the service. When they started to sing "Amazing Grace" in Japanese, my eyes watered up with joy as the Holy Spirit bore witness to their heart of worship. Being around other believers worshiping was completely uplifting. The pastor let me share what I was doing with the group, and I was received with open arms.

As soon as the service was over, two of the women from the congregation, Naoko and Miyuki, handed me twenty-two dollars. Once again, I had never asked for money, but through the LORD providing, I now had forty-four dollars in my pocket. This was more money than I normally carried on me at home. One of the other women invited me to stay at her house with her and her husband. I was thrilled to have a place to stay, especially now knowing how dangerous the Nashville bus station was advertised to be. Unfortunately, these precious people lived too far away, and I wouldn't have been able to make it back to the bus station in time to catch my next bus. She seemed genuinely heartbroken, as she had offered to help me and due to the distance could not.

The pastor came over to me and offered me the use of the shower located in the recreation room if I would like to take one. There was one small catch, however. The recreation room shower had no towels. With a big grin on my face, I said, "That would be great; thank you." I took my shower, and the hot water and soap were great. I felt refreshed and renewed. I couldn't recall the last time I felt each individual drop coming down. It was as if I had never really appreciated or thanked God for having a shower in my house. The absence of the normal comforts of home changed my attitude and my gratitude for them. Then it was time to dry off using paper from the paper towel dispenser that featured the brown paper bag material we have all used on occasion. I didn't mind at all that pieces of the paper towel were sticking all over my body. I felt like a brown mummy in some low-budget horror film. I laughed as I peeled most of the pieces off and got dressed in my change of clothes.

After getting dressed, the new and improved William left and talked to more people. The results were more of the same, but I noticed my attitude was one of thanksgiving and not of discouragement.

I headed back to the church to attend the regular six o'clock evening service. Before it began, I was able to speak to the executive pastor. I explained that I was hoping the church would be able to help with what I really needed, which at that point was a bed. He told me that pizza was being served after the service for a dollar a slice and if I wanted to, I could take advantage of that. I felt like I was asking for an apple and he said, "Here, have an orange." I did not complain at all. I just said, "Thank you; that would be nice." I started to notice a theme with some of the leadership at these churches I was visiting in regard to their willingness to help someone in need. It seemed that they simply did not want to be bothered. It was disheartening to see that some pastors just didn't want to put forth any effort to a brother in need, even one that was there in their own city to share the gospel.

That night, the youth choir provided the entire evening service, and they did an amazing job. After the service, there was pizza and ice cream, and I purchased one slice of pizza. I sat with Pastor Barry's wife and their two adopted Japanese children. She extended the same kind of kindness her husband had shared just hours earlier.

I approached the senior pastor, since he was not there earlier in the day, about what I was doing and shared my need for a place to sleep. He said, "I am sorry, but the best I could do is get you into a public shelter." When he said those words, his body language was confusing. I couldn't tell if he had the means but not the time or that he just didn't have anything. He smiled with a half grin as though he was putting me up in a five-star diamond hotel.

I was saddened that once again I was just being shown the door, but this time I was secure in the LORD. "My bus is leaving around four in the morning; will the shelter allow me to leave early in order to get there?"

"No. I would offer to get you a hotel, but everything is booked because of the music festival," he said, looking around the room at the other people. I didn't feel as though I had his full attention. I wondered how he knew that there was no room, not even one bed available. It seemed like an empty offer.

"I understand; thank you. Can you point me toward the bus station?"

We left the social event and walked outside together, where he said, "I would have you stay at my house, but

I just got back in town today. I wasn't even supposed to be here. The reason I came back early was because my son was in the group that was singing tonight." For the first time I was being talked to with a genuine and sincere face. He was looking me right in the eyes and didn't have that half smile anymore.

His words and actions reminded me of my own father coming back from his trip early in order to see me off. Unlike the church the day before and his executive pastor earlier, I could see the sincerity from him and could tell there was some sadness from him due to his seeming inability to help me. He walked with me for about two blocks and then pointed me in the direction of the public shelter and the bus station. Before leaving, I looked at the pastor and humbly asked him, "If I might say two things before I go?" He assured me I could. "Pastor, if I was your son, would you want me to spend the night at that shelter?"

The pastor hung his head and said, "No."

"If your son came to our church and shared a need for food and shelter, what would you want us to do for him?" With his head still looking down, the pastor said nothing. As I started to walk away, I looked back at the pastor and said, "Pastor, I believe that if you could help me, you would. I just want to encourage you the next time a brother or sister in Christ comes to your city for the express purpose of proclaiming the good news of the gospel of Christ, you will go beyond what is convenient and do everything you can for them."

As the pastor nodded, I started to walk to the bus station—the very bus station I had been told was the most dangerous station in the entire South. I started to sing aloud, "I have decided to follow Jesus, though none go with me I still will follow, the world behind me, His cross before me, no turning back, no turning back." Amazingly, I had transformed from being scared and timid the day before to a lion chaser. God was doing a work in my heart.

THEOLOGICAL
BUS STOP

Walking into the bus station, I could see that there were a lot of people just hanging out. It was larger than either of the other two bus stations I had been in, and as I looked around, I spotted a group of young twenty-somethings and asked if I could join them. One of the girls said, "Sure. My name is Angelissa. Join the random group." She was referring to a group of individuals that happened to be waiting for their buses and just decided to sit with one another. Angelissa was a heavyset young lady with long black hair and appeared to have a great confidence as she led the conversations for the most part. The other two people never shared their names and didn't say much the entire time I was there. Within minutes of my talking to them about Jesus, two of them got up and walked away. This didn't bother me since I was getting used to people walking away from me after hearing the name of Jesus. It is very easy to bring Jesus up immediately in a conversation when everything you are doing at that moment in your life is about sharing Him with others.

When the questions came about why I was there or what I was doing, I responded that it was all about Jesus.

Angelissa had a bunch of different questions and shared with me that she was attending a school that was affiliated with the Church of Christ. She started to ask me personal conviction questions, and I told her that I would share with her what I believed and why I believed it. I figured, since it was the two questions I was hoping to ask everyone else, I should be willing to answer the same questions of what and why.

"Is baptism part of salvation?" she asked. I responded by saying that I believe baptism is an outward expression of an inward decision. It is something that takes place after someone surrenders their life to Jesus Christ and not before. I believe that all who are called children of God should be baptized out of obedience but not unto salvation. The criminal that was crucified next to Christ didn't have the opportunity to be baptized after Jesus told him he would "remember him." There is also nothing to imply that this same thief was baptized before going on the cross either.

She then asked, "Is homosexuality a worse sin than others?" I explained that having the temptation to act on homosexuality is not a sin. Acting on that temptation is a sin, just as it would be if a heterosexual man were to lust and have sex with a woman outside of marriage. I went on to explain to her that my own aunt has a homosexual lifestyle and in spite of that I love her and treat her no differently than any other family member. I told her I personally didn't understand the anger that some Christians have toward homosexuals, as their sin is no greater than anyone else's.

She then commented that she had been told to teach young people at the school to speak in tongues but that she herself didn't believe in speaking in tongues. She asked me what she should do. I encouraged her to not do anything that she didn't feel at peace with God about. Not everyone, I explained, who will enter the kingdom of heaven will have the same theology or doctrine. Better to be true to the Spirit of God in your life than with tradition or what others might tell you in conflict with God's leading. I told her that I had my own convictions, which were based on my understanding of what the Bible teaches and not the opinion of society or changing whims of the culture. I encouraged her to do the same in every area of her life. She smiled, and then we prayed together for safe travels and for clear conviction from God. She was a very sweet young woman, and it was apparent to me that she had a true desire to serve the LORD. As she left to get on her bus, I thanked the LORD for the opportunity to minister to her, and I looked for someone else to talk to.

I noticed a young man sitting down reading a small book, and then he slipped into some form of deep meditation. He looked as though he could have been a professional surfer. He was Caucasian with long, blond, curly hair and very tan. Out of respect, I waited for him to be done, and then I went over to him. "Excuse me," I said, "I couldn't help but notice you over here. Are you okay?"

He nodded and said, "Yes, I was just praying."

"What faith do you practice, if you don't mind my asking?"

"No, not at all. I believe in the Bahai faith."

"I've never heard of that before. Do you mind telling me more about it?" After introducing myself and finding out his name was Justin, he explained to me that it was a religion that was formed in Iran in 1844. Justin did not look like he was Iranian at all. In fact, he had a New Zealand accent and looked like a surfer, with his blond hair and tan skin.

He said, "The Bahai faith believes that there is one God and that all religions and religious books are correct, written in different times for different people."

Though I'm no expert on any religion, including my own, what he was saying sounded confusing to me. Not knowing anything about his religion, I figured I would ask him some basic questions. "If it is true that all religions are correct, do they contradict themselves in any way?"

"No."

"Then can you explain to me how Buddhism teaches there is no God, Hinduism teaches there are over three hundred gods, and Judaism believes there is one God?"

At that moment, he looked as if my question had caught him off guard. "They do?"

With a slight smile, I said, "Yes, they do."

He then tried to explain that the Bible is truth but equal to other religious writings and that there are many ways to heaven.

I asked, "If what you are telling me is true, how can the Bible be truth and Jesus claim that He is the only way to heaven and that no one can come to the Father, which is where heaven is, but through Him? This can be found in John 14:6." Evidently he didn't know, because he said nothing. I followed up that question with, "Now that was widely about religions as a whole, but you also said their books and teachings don't contradict as well. Is that correct?" Not meaning to be argumentative, I asked if he could explain to me how Islam's book, the Quran, teaches that Jesus Christ was a prophet but not God himself or even the Son of God, in complete contrast to what the Bible clearly teaches regarding Jesus as God's only Son and that He, Jesus, was also God. Again, he really was at a loss for words.

We exchanged e-mail addresses and encouraged each other to do some additional research regarding each other's religion. Even though I didn't fully understand or know much about his beliefs, I knew what mine were. This young guy was very nice and respectful. He said to me, "I have some Christian friends that are good people. But you are the first one I didn't know that encouraged me to seek the face of God and did not tell me that I was just going to hell. I can tell that you really live out what you believe, and I respect that." I thanked him for his words, and then he left to get on his bus.

It was now two thirty in the morning, and I was again looking for someone else to talk to. About two benches down from where Justin and I were talking, I noticed an elderly man that was sitting by himself. He seemed saddened; it was evident in the lack of both color in his face and the frown that was apparent.

Amos, an eighty-three-year-old man, began to share with me that he attended a Presbyterian church back in Knoxville. He was coming back from his wife's memorial service. He said, "I married a Smith, and she died after twenty-seven years of marriage; and then I happened to marry another Smith, and she died after twenty-eight years of marriage." He explained that he was okay with where God had him and that he would see both of his wives again in heaven one day. I could tell that he was at peace with the passing of his wife and that other than being tired due to the time, he was actually joyful.

As he continued to share, he said, "It wasn't a sudden death, and because of that, you want your loved one to go as quickly and as painlessly as possible."

"What happens if you get home and you meet a woman with the last name Smith? What would you do?"

He smiled. "If the LORD leads, then I say okay." Then he chuckled and said, "Come to think of it, I will probably run the other way." Here was a man that just lost not his first but his second wife. By the way he talked about her, I could tell that he really loved her and missed her greatly. In spite of this, there was nothing but joy shining from him because his faith was in Christ, and he knew that she was in a place where she had no more pain. I was encouraged, and even though I missed my wife and kids, I asked God to give me the same courage and peace that Amos had. Just like those before him, he got on his bus, and I again looked for someone to talk to. I went outside the bus station, where some homeless people were gathered. After sitting with them for a while, with most of them just sleeping or keeping to themselves, I headed back inside, as it was now close to my bus departure time.

It was close to 4:00 a.m. I noticed that the LORD had protected me through the evening. While I was talking in the restaurant area with my newfound friends, there had been about a half-dozen police officers that came in to do a drug raid. No shots were fired, but some people were arrested, according to the security guard on duty. Not only was I safe, but I was unaware of what was going on around me. I was just focused on listening and sharing with the people I came into contact with. My bus arrived on time, and once on board, I choose to sleep for the two-and-half-hour ride to Louisville, Kentucky, so my body could get some rest.

HOLY
LOUISVILLE

Surprisingly, I woke up from what was more like a nap than actual sleep with full energy. As soon as I stepped off the bus, an elderly man handed me something, said, "Here is some food for the soul," and walked away. I looked down at the little piece of paper that was in my hand and noticed a cross on it. I ran after the man and asked if we could talk. We introduced ourselves. He was a sixty-year-plus Caucasian man standing about five feet nine inches, with glasses and a little hat. Ergy explained to me that he didn't live in the city but would travel in from time to time in order to share God's word. "I live about an hour away," he said, "and I attend a church there. This is just something I like to do." I smiled and shared with him why I was there. Ergy prayed with me and gave me ten dollars for lunch. I didn't want money, but Ergy wanted to make sure I would get something to eat. He continued to walk around to share with other people.

Once again, the LORD was providing my every need, and in my heart I knew that this day was going to be awesome. Already pumped up from seeing another Christian out sharing his faith and wanting to serve, I sat down and read my next "Letter of Paul." Dr. Tony Foglio, a retired senior pastor from San Diego, wrote these words to me:

> Ryan,
>
> Thank you for asking me to write this note. It is as if I am with you on your journey. I pray that your mission is going well. I am sure that it is, because "The LORD makes firm the steps of the one who delights in him" (Psalm 37:23, NIV).
>
> Be patient with those that you meet today. Be slow to judge either good or bad. Be slow to shake the dust from your feet. Good people do not always have understanding—the person(s) who may turn you away just might be going through even a more difficult time than you. Bless them (Romans 12:14–15).
>
>> Consider it pure joy, my brothers and sisters, whenever you face trials of many kinds, because you know that the testing of your faith produces perseverance.
>>
>> James 1:2–3 (NIV)
>
>> If someone wishes to bless you with good things, be thankful. If someone invites you into their home, be a gracious guest.
>>
>> Matthew 10:11–14

If asked what you are doing, answer clearly. Keep a skip in your step and a smile on your face. You have been blessed by God's calling.

1 Peter 3:15

Do not be afraid to enjoy your journey.

Make many friends by showing yourself friendly.

A couple more verses for you today: Acts 5:41–42.

I am praying with and for you and your family.

Your friend,

Tony Foglio

PS: If you're in the Midwest and are treated to a White Castle hamburger, think of me.

Keeping those words of wisdom in mind, I headed toward the Walnut Street Baptist Church. I loved reading these letters; each one gave me the push I needed. *The steps of a good man are ordered by the* LORD echoed in my heart as I walked. I didn't want to be on a trip that I wanted but what God wanted. I hoped that I wouldn't be treated to White Castle or a Krystal since I don't personally care for their food. However, if I was asked to eat there, I would and be grateful for it.

Arriving at the beautiful stone church, I noticed the church doors were locked. Then, from a side door, a woman came out. She pointed me to the church office. There I was able to talk to the business administrator, Harold, and share what I needed. He offered me a couch at the church to stay at. Finally, a church was willing to let me sleep after two nights in a bus stop and outside with homeless people. I was thrilled. I asked if I could have some invitation cards from the church so that I could hand them out to people I met with. Moved by what I was doing, he took me upstairs, where the church staff was having their weekly meeting.

There were eleven staff members sitting around their conference table. I was a little overwhelmed with the audience that was before me. It appeared that the setting was one of great importance. I felt all their eyes on me as I stood with my pack in hand. Harold politely interrupted the senior pastor and said, "There is a young man here. I think you should hear what he is doing." A smile came over the man at the end of the table, Senior Pastor Rusty Ellison.

Without hesitation, Pastor Ellison allowed me to share with the staff what I was doing. I talked for about fifteen minutes and began to weep. I shared about missing my family and the failure in Chattanooga to the experience I had in Nashville and how excited I was when I met Ergy. I thanked Pastor Ellison for allowing me to share as well as letting me stay there at the church. "You are the first church that has opened their doors to me. Selfishly, I expected all churches to do so, but only you have. Thank you, thank you."

As I was finishing up my story, I noticed that Pastor Ellison leaned over to the youth pastor, Kris Billiter, and whispered something to him, which prompted him to start typing on his laptop.

I could see that all of the women were touched, especially when I mentioned about my family. A few of the men were whispering to one another. Pastor Ellison said,

"I am very proud of you, and I think it is great what you are doing. I know you must love your family very much, but you will be even a better husband and father when you return because you are falling more in love with Christ, and I am excited for you."

Pastor Billiter asked while still typing, "Would you like to stay closer to the bus station?"

With the front of my shirt becoming soaked as the tears fell so rapidly, I said, "That would be great since my bus is really early. But I do not mind walking back from the church." My bus was going to be boarding around four in the morning, and the church was a couple of miles away, but I could not pass up on shelter for the evening. The whole staff came and laid hands on me and prayed over me. The youth pastor gave me a granola bar because he wanted to give all that I was asking for. He told me that the hotel room was on the church and not to worry about anything. The church provided everything I had requested and even more. With the address of the hotel in hand and food for the day in my bag, I was overwhelmed with the love that this body of believers showed to me.

When leaving, he told me about how the Southern Baptist Convention was going to be in the city the following week and that there were some youth groups there and they were out doing street evangelism. I was so excited I headed down the street.

Walking with a pep in my step, I came up to three men sitting in a courtyard. They were not sitting together but about twenty feet apart from one another. Each man was involved in himself in some form or another. The first man was an older black man reading a newspaper and smoking a cigarette.

The second was a mid-forties black man appearing to be in deep thought. The last man was a mid-twenties Caucasian listening to music on his iPod and just rocking out. Sitting outside the public library, each man had his own bench and tree for company. I approached the first man, and when I went to introduce myself and hand him a tract, he literally shunned me away, waving his hand for me to go. I smiled and turned to the second man. I handed him a tract and said, "Please take a moment and read this over; I will be right back."

Just as I was heading over to give a tract to the third person, the second man said, "Excuse me, are you a pastor or something?"

I found it interesting that he assumed I was a pastor of some sort since I was handing out the Good News. I turned and walked back to him. "No, not really. Just a Christian sharing the truth of Christ."

He then spoke with someberness in his voice. "Will you pray with me?"

I was humbled and excited for the opportunity to talk to God with him. I sat down next to him. "Of course I can. What is it you would like for me to pray with you about?"

He put his head down and said something I had never heard before. In fact, I had never even heard of a pastor dealing with this issue. He said, "I am struggling with the temptation to molest children."

I was taken aback at first and didn't know exactly how to respond. After pausing for a second, though it felt like an hour, I said, "Sir, I have to ask you up front, have you ever acted on this temptation?" He said no and went on to explain to me his struggle and how it had never gone past inappropriate behavior with himself. As he shared his story,

I couldn't help but ask God, "What would you have me do?" I whispered that to God as he continued with his problems.

He said, "I know it is wrong and that it is a sin, but I can feel my mind-set getting worse. I have never told anyone about this before, and I have been struggling with this for a long time now. When you handed me this card, I felt like screaming out to you. I am scared and I need help."

I could tell that he was sincere and that this was something that was greatly weighing on his heart. At that moment, I was thinking, *Who comes right out and shares their darkest and most shameful problem in their life with a complete stranger?*

I looked at him and said, "Let's pray." As I prayed with him, I could tell that he truly needed help. I asked God to give this man the strength to seek Him first in all things. I then prayed for the man to be given courage to go speak to a professional counselor for help and accountability. I requested the LORD to restore the joy of his salvation and to give him peace that this struggle would not have to paralyze him anymore. Though before we started praying I was asking God to give me direction on how to help this man, praying for him was a glorious experience. It was not hard at all to lift up a person who was suffering or struggling and make their requests to God.

This was the first time I had ever been approached with the issue of child molestation. I had never even heard of a pastor or another Christian being in that situation before. Though it was different for me, it was the same to God.

After we finished praying, he said, "Thank you for caring for me enough to stop and pray."

"I will always pray with anyone who is in need. However, prayer is not enough for what you are going through. I know this was difficult for you to share with a stranger, but what you need is accountability and counseling." I told him of Walnut Street Baptist and gave him a card with their information on it. "Go there and talk to a pastor. If they are unequipped to help you, I believe that they will care enough to do all they can to get you the help you are needing."

He smiled and said, "Thank you, and I will." I was amazed at how people will share their most sensitive issues in their life if someone will first take the time to love them not because of who they are but whose they are. I was amazed by how in God's sovereign will the two of us spoke to each other. In my plan I wouldn't have been in that city at that time and been able to talk to that man about his problem and pray with him. In John 14 Jesus claims that those who love Him will obey Him. I realized that it isn't a calling to go love one another and share the gospel but one of obedience.

As I walked a couple of blocks, I noticed an elderly man sitting on a bench. He appeared to be in his late seventies. Very tan, there was a possibility he was Native American. I asked him if I could join him, and he said, "It's a free bench."

Sitting down, I said, "My name is William; what is yours?"

"Raymond," he said with a smile on his face. I could tell he was happy someone acknowledged him and would stop to talk with him.

"Well, Raymond, we are truly blessed with some beautiful weather today. Just another example of what only God can do. Do you believe in God?"

He looked down at first into his folded hands and then back at me. "I believe that there is a superior power of some kind, but I don't know if it is God or nature."

"Do you mind telling me what it is you believe and why?"

"No, not at all. I'm a self-taught man. I love to go to the library and read everything and anything. I'm retired now and on a fixed income, so the library allows me to explore without spending money. I believe that when we die, we just stop existing. There is nothing after life, as there is no proof of there being anything after we die."

His answer was so sad and hopeless. If that were true, then there would be no purpose as to why life exists. I needed to know what this educated man thought about the only way to hope. "Who do you think Jesus Christ was?"

"A good man like Gandhi or Martin Luther King Jr."

I smiled slightly because I had heard this argument before. "Do you think someone who could be known as being a good man could also be a notorious liar?"

"No, he wouldn't be considered a very good man, would he?" He made hand gestures in the air, as if to throw a ball or in this case the notion of a good man being a liar, and turned his head away from me.

"Well, Jesus claimed the only way to God was through Him. Now, if He wasn't a liar, then he must be telling the truth." I could see on his face that he didn't know how to respond. I continued by saying, "Do you really believe that there is neither a heaven nor a hell?"

He surprised me with his answer. "If they do exist, then I would rather go to hell so others can go to heaven."

I was taken aback at first by his response. "Raymond, if you go to hell, no one would go to heaven in your place. There is not a capacity limit on the number of people who will be entering the kingdom of God, but He's the only one who knows what that final number will be, as it is still being added to every day. Your proposal sounds noble, but in reality, nobody's life would benefit by you choosing to go to hell."

"If God really wants me to go to heaven, then He is going to have to tell me!" With slight aspiration on his face, he now was looking me right in the eyes. I could see that he was struggling with the line of fact and faith. His knowledge wouldn't allow him to move, but Jesus was knocking on his heart.

"He did," I explained. "Through His word and through the life of His Son, Jesus Christ."

While I was explaining this to him, a Hispanic man came up to me and asked me for a nickel. I agreed to give him one but then realized I didn't have any change. Raymond ignored the man's request, so I gave the man a dollar bill. He offered to give me his ninety-five cents in return, but I told him he could keep it. He was very thankful and walked away. Raymond got upset and said, "You support scammers and lazy people. If he wants money, he needs to get a job. I worked my whole life, and now I am on a fixed income. I don't have any money to give to people who aren't willing to work for it."

I calmly responded. "Raymond, he asked for a nickel. He could only ask for four less cents than he did. I don't knowingly support scammers. I do, however, try to show compassion, and if someone is in need and I can help, I do so." At that moment, the Hispanic man came out of the store across from where we were sitting, eating some food he had just purchased. In my heart, I was glad that the man had used the money on food. At that point, I asked Raymond if I could pray with him.

He responded by saying, "Can I pray for you first?" I was surprised by the request since he didn't believe in God. I thought for a moment and wanted to hear what a faithless prayer to a disbelief god sounded like. I nodded yes, and we both bowed our heads. "Oh great universe, please protect this young man on his travel. Thank you for today's weather, and may it continue." And with that, he was done with his prayer.

I prayed, "Dear heavenly Father, thank you for life. Thank you for Raymond and bringing us together today. I pray that you will reveal your truth to him today. I ask that he will come to believe and receive you as his LORD and Savior. Please continue to guide our paths, and may you be pleased by how we conduct our lives. I love you and thank you for your Son and the sacrifice, burial and resurrection He made, not only for me, but for Raymond as well. In Christ's Holy and precious name I pray with full confidence that you hear my prayer, amen."

We stood and shook hands. As we did, Raymond reached into his pocket and handed me a five-dollar bill. "Raymond, what is this for?"

"Lunch."

"I thought you were on a fixed income and wouldn't give money to anyone who didn't earn it."

With a smile on his face, he said, "I believe in what it is you are doing, and I just want to help."

"Thank you for the money, but believe in what I am saying more than what I am doing."

He smiled again and said he would think about it. As I left him, I decided I would walk to the hotel so I could drop off my bag and soak my feet for a few minutes. I had not been on my feet for such a long time, and my body was getting weak and sore.

I didn't have the name of the hotel, just the address. After about twenty minutes of walking around trying to find it, I was still lost. Being downtown, there were businesses and tall buildings all around me. I asked a man for directions, and he pointed me to around the corner. I held my breath as I stopped and looked up at the twenty-five-story building standing before me. The name of the hotel was the Galt House.

As I entered into the spectacular lobby, I thought to myself that it must be a five-star resort hotel. The hotel was on both sides of the street, with a private bridge connecting them. The doorman opened the door and greeted me. Several valet attendants were on call, with a bellman ready for the bags of the next arriving guests. I was now thinking it was a six-star hotel. I kept thinking, *I must have the wrong address*. In spite of this, I decided I would check at the desk and see if there was a reservation with my name on it. I walked up to the counter and said, "Hello, I don't know if I have a reservation here or not. My last name is Rebold."

The young lady behind the counter typed my name in her computer. "Mr. Rebold, we do have a room for you, and though it is located in our other tower, I can check you in here." I don't know if she noticed my mouth drop to the ground, but I was shocked.

Once I picked my mouth off the ground, I thought about how my clothes smelled. I was hoping I could change that scent of adventure with more of a fresh spring aroma. "Do you have washing machines here?"

"We have a laundry service that you can use. You can receive your clothes back by 6:00 a.m. the next morning." Unfortunately, my next bus was scheduled to leave at 4:00 a.m. again, so that was not going to work.

As I walked into my room, I couldn't help grinning from ear to ear. Once again, my eyes filled with tears of joy as a result of realizing how much love the pastoral staff of Walnut Street Baptist Church had expressed to me. Once again, God had proven Himself faithful. The room was amazing, with a big soft bed that looked like a handpicked cloud for my sore body. The granite countertops were speckled black, and the bathtub was calling my name. I hadn't stayed in that many high-priced hotels before, so I felt as if there was royalty in the area and I was being treated as such. I couldn't believe how much I missed the basic accommodations. It is amazing what a pillow can do for someone who has gone without. I was very excited, knowing I was going to be able to get some good rest later that night.

I unloaded my bag and soaked my feet in the bathtub for about ten minutes. I knew I couldn't stay any longer or I would just stay in the comforts of this blessing. Even the simple thing of just soaking my feet in water changed my physical, emotional, and spiritual mood. Though the water was restoring, I knew I had a job to do. I didn't want this gift to be abused or on false pretenses, so I dried off my feet and got ready to go out again.

Before leaving to go out and be a witness again, I looked back over the letters I had already read and the challenges I hadn't yet completed. I decided to read another letter for the sake of another challenge. *Be patient and lean not on my own understanding* was still ringing in my ear. I felt as if I was slowly being taken off of my itinerary and being put on one designed by God. Chuck Morris, the executive pastor at Chilhowee Hills Baptist Church in Knoxville, Tennessee, where I attend, wrote this to me:

Ryan,

I'm not sure which day it is that you are reading this, but whichever one it is, you can trust that God is with you. You are either near the beginning of a great journey or in the midst of it, but either way, I know it's exciting! Since I can't pray for you only on the day you are reading this letter (because I don't know the exact day!), I'll simply have to pray every day.

The challenge I feel led to present to you for this day is to perform one act of service for some person who seems as though they *don't* need it. In other words, see if you can find someone who appears to be better off than you: well-dressed, clean, employed, or any other descriptive term that would seem to be the opposite of what you are portraying during the week. (I am assuming that most of the people you will talk to this week would be the down-and-out or those who may be on the streets.) The challenge would be to see if you are able to reach *up* across the societal boundaries to serve someone else with the intent of presenting the gospel to them. In fact, you may find an opportunity to tell them your story. Just imagine if God were to lead you to a book publisher or some other miraculous encounter that would make your trip's impact expand beyond the actual week!

Don't limit yourself to reaching out to certain members of society; look today for an unlikely candidate and serve them purposefully! You may very well have the chance to impact the life of a person who appears to have all the answers. But we all know that riches are temporal, and material things are phony dividing lines between otherwise equal human beings. Paul wrote to Timothy about what to tell rich people:

> Command those who are rich in this present world not to be arrogant nor to put their hope in wealth, which is so uncertain, but to put their hope in God, who richly provides us with everything for our enjoyment. Command them to do good, to be rich in good deeds, and to be generous and willing to share. In this way they will lay up treasure for themselves as a firm foundation for the coming age, so that they may take hold of the life that is truly life.
>
> 1 Timothy 6:17–19 (NIV)

I trust that God's good hand is upon you as you walk with Him this week!

Pastor Chuck Morris

I was encouraged by the words that Pastor Chuck wrote for me. Once again I was humbled by the time that someone whom I respect would take to help me on my trip. Looking at his unique challenge for me, I realized that I needed to stop looking at the obvious people in need and step out and look to help someone who was not in need in a financial sense.

There was something within my psyche about going to businesspeople in suits or young people with the appearance of money that made it difficult for me to talk to them. I thought that people who seemed to have some apparent need were more inclined to listen to a stranger because of their situation. However, people with money need Jesus just as much, and for those reasons I was excited for this new challenge. I wanted to see if I could help someone that wasn't in need like the majority of people I had talked to. I wondered exactly who or where such an encounter would happen, but nonetheless, I was motivated to fulfill this challenge.

Heading out again, I needed to go to a Laundromat to buy some detergent. My plan was to wash my clothes in the hotel sink and let them air-dry overnight. I found out that the closest Laundromat was several miles away, so I decided to take a trolley ride for fifty cents. While it was making some stops along the way, a familiar face got on. It was my new friend Raymond.

He smiled and said, "You will never believe what happened to me. After we finished talking with each other, I went to my bank to open a savings account. They told me in order to do that I would need to pay the bank $35 a month. As I was sitting in the bank filling out the paperwork, one of the bank employees asked me to go with them. I followed them into the bank manager's office, where the manager proceeds to tell me they are going to waive the monthly fee since I have been a loyal customer." He was very excited by this news.

"That's great, Raymond. I am happy for you." I was excited that God had blessed him with that savings. I didn't know what he thought about the blessing, though.

He then added, "I know the reason why that happened to me. It is because I gave you that five dollars. I gave and therefore I was given to."

It seemed as if he was leaning toward some sort of karma perspective, so I said, "That is great. Each of us should give to one another, but not with the hope of receiving something in return. I believe because you gave out of a heart of compassion, you were blessed by God in return. It wasn't the act of giving but the heart of the giver."

He smiled. "I like that."

Arriving at Raymond's stop first, I once again encouraged him to put his faith in Christ. "We aren't promised tomorrow, so don't pillow your head tonight without accepting Jesus Christ as your Savior."

He smiled and said, "I am still thinking about everything. Thank you for caring. Be safe."

I arrived at the Laundromat, but I couldn't wash my laundry there, as I would be sitting there in my birthday suit while my clothes were being washed. I didn't think that would bring glory to God, so I bought a small box of soap and headed out.

I came up to a food court in what looked like an outdoor mall and decided to buy something to eat. I realize that some people might not think that food from Taco Bell would be the best choice for someone who hadn't eaten very much for several days, but I was craving a chicken Baja Gordita and an ice-cold Mountain Dew.

Walking up to the restaurant, I noticed a group of young people all wearing the same kind of T-shirts. They were members of the youth group that the staff at Walnut Street Baptist Church had told me about. Thinking of Pastor Chuck's letter, I decided to help someone who wasn't in obvious need. I thought about pretending to be a lost person in an effort to challenge a young person and really test their faith and belief. I waited for one of them to be by themselves, and then I made my move.

I had just sat down to eat my food when I noticed one of the young men from the group standing in line a few feet from me. I took this as the moment. "Excuse me," I said. "What is with all the matching shirts? Are you all a part of a club or something?"

He walked over to where I was. The young man was built as either a football player or a wrestler. He had dark brown hair that came down over his face and then to the side, similar to Justin Bieber's style. As he walked over closer to where I was, he didn't seem to be intimidated by talking to a stranger. With a smile on his face, he said, "No. We are all involved with the same youth group."

"What are you doing here?"

"We are just in the city for the day telling people about Jesus." Making complete eye contact and slightly smiling, he was now standing right next to me. He appeared to be happy about the present opportunity to talk.

I paused for a moment and then asked, "Are you one of those Christian people?"

"Yes, I am."

"Tell me why you believe in Jesus."

His face changed to business mode. Looking determined, he spent the next five minutes sharing with me why he felt it was important to believe in Jesus. I thought he did a great job in speaking from his heart, but I wanted to see how he would respond to someone who disliked what he was saying. So I said, "Your God cannot be very loving if he makes people go to hell. How is that love?"

He took that comment as if he was a boxer that just took a serious body hit. He paused and gathered his thoughts for a moment. "Everyone has the opportunity to enter heaven; it is their choice to believe or not."

We continued back and forth for about ten minutes with me grilling him and him coming right back at me with good, solid responses. He shared how his mother had been healed from cancer and how only God could have done so. I paused for a second and went at him hard, saying, "My mother died of cancer. Where was your healing God then?"

He looked at me and said very sincerely, "I am sorry about your mother."

Finally, I felt like it was time for me to let him know who I really was. Even at the most heated time in our discussion, this young man never lost his composure. That impressed me because I have seen grown men yelling at someone who didn't listen or agree with what they were saying. I stopped him in midsentence and said, "I am proud of you."

He didn't understand why I would say that. "What do you mean?"

"I am a Christian. I am here today doing the same thing you are. I wanted to test you, as iron sharpens iron, to see how you would respond to someone who didn't just calmly listen to you."

He was surprised. "I just wanted you to hear why you needed Jesus."

I also told him my mother was alive and that was just part of my character. I asked for forgiveness if I had offended him in any way.

He smiled and said, "Not at all."

At this point, one of his youth leaders came over and joined us, and I shared with both of them what it was I was doing there. I ate half of my food during our encounter, and my appetite was gone. The young man then asked me for advice on how to approach people and if there were different methods to witnessing. He expressed a genuine desire to go out and share the gospel with people, and that just fueled my passion to get out and do some more witnessing myself. The three of us walked down the street, and I shared what little wisdom I had on witnessing. I gave him a handful of my tracts and told him how I used them mainly for conversation starters.

As we were walking, I noticed during my conversation with the leader that the young man was no longer with us. We stopped and turned around, and about ten feet behind us, we saw the young man. He had stopped and was giving a card and sharing Jesus with two people that had just passed by us.

I told the youth leader, "I wish when I was seventeen I would have had the same passion and the drive that he does."

He responded, saying, "I can't even do what he does."

A few minutes later, the young man rejoined us with a big smile. "What else can you teach me?"

As we turned and walked a few blocks farther, we came up to their bus. There was now a large group of young people standing outside, and some of this young man's friends came over to where we were. He said, "Tell them what you are doing. You guys have to hear this." I shared what I was doing, and when I had finished, he said, "I hope one day I can be courageous enough to do what you are doing." Wow. I was flattered and felt even more compelled to complete all of the challenges I had received in my "Letters of Paul." I prayed that his light would continue to get brighter and that he would desire to follow Christ more and more each day. I said good-bye and watched as he and his friends boarded their bus.

As I turned and walked down the street, I believed I had been inspired much more by this young man than anything I could have done for him. I remembered Galatians 6:10 reads, "Therefore, as we have opportunity, let us do good to all people, especially to those who belong to the family of believers" (NIV).

While walking, I came across a bagman who seemed to be somewhat deranged. He was talking to himself out loud, and somehow he wasn't in agreement within himself. He was a shorter, skinny, black man with a lot of carts around him that were filled with random things. After leaving the youth group, I was pumped up to talk to anyone and everyone. This man just happened to be next in my path.

He said that he had not sinned in five years and that he was called by God to sue the city. He told me he was making a movie about his life at that moment, even though there was no visible equipment. He explained to me that I was unable to see the cameras. He said he believed he had been anointed by God but felt there was no need to teach or preach since Jesus never commanded us to do so.

I felt so much sorrow for this man. I didn't think about the situation of his mental state and just cared that he didn't understand the truth. The Bible is written for everyone, but there are sections of the Bible that separate the reader by time, culture, and covenant, and these factors, if misread, can confuse anyone. Parts of Scripture are also written in different ways, such as literal, metaphorical, and descriptive. It seemed as though this man just read parts of the Bible and took them for what he believed to be true. Truth must be consistent within itself, and therefore the Bible cannot contradict itself.

Though I did not know how someone could explain the great commission without preaching or teaching, rather than debate that issue, I chose to confront him about repentance of sin. After discussing repentance with him, he told me he believed there was no reason for him to repent, since he had gone for such a long time without sinning. I asked him if he had lied within the past five years, and he said, "Yes. But lying is not a sin." Since that didn't seem to faze him, I followed that up by asking him if he had ever stolen anything or looked at women with sexual desire. He said, "Yes. But I didn't steal anything big, and I am just admiring the beautiful canvasses that God has made."

Learning this process from "The Way of The Master," I explained to him how he had broken God's law. I went on to explain that he needed to repent from those sins and what it really meant to be born again. He responded by saying that these truths didn't apply to him since he was already anointed and was on a different level than me. It was at this point that I realized I couldn't get this man to reason with me because his thought process was just too irrational. I gave him a card, wished him well, and walked down the street. It began to rain, and the streets were becoming bare.

As I was walking around a corner, I spotted a hot dog vendor. He was taller than six feet and had one of those safari hardhats on. He was standing under his multicolor umbrella that was covering his entire stand, trying to stay dry. He was the next person that was on the street that I was walking on, so I chose to go over to him. I walked over and sat on a bench right next to him. I asked him if he had any kids, and he shared with me that he had a little girl but didn't see her very much because he and his girlfriend had been separated for some time. He told me he was a Christian and that he felt his life was like the story of Job. I asked, "Are you mad at God?"

He seemed to be getting a little heated by the question I asked. If it wasn't for the steam from the hot dogs, you would think he was the one steaming."Yes, I am. I don't feel like I can catch a break. Why can't God just bring me some good things in my life for a change? You bet I am mad at Him. I am angry." I could tell that he definitely had some issues that he was struggling with in his life. However, it didn't seem that his attitude was anything like Job's.

"I don't know if you remember the complete story of Job. Satan had gone up to heaven and basically challenged God that he could get anyone to turn from Him. God asked Satan if he had considered His servant Job. God told Satan that he couldn't take his life, and in spite of all kinds of devastating events introduced into Job's life, Satan was unable to cause Job to lose his faith. After losing all of his kids, his belongings, and his health, he still didn't get mad at God. Based on what I have heard you say, it sounds as if your attitude is completely opposite of Job's."

He looked down at his cart for a moment. "You're right. I have been blaming God for my bad choices." I asked him if he had ever repented of his sins or changed his life in order to live for Christ. "No. I don't even know what you are talking about."

I asked him to share with me what made him a Christian.

"I believe that Jesus was the Son of God and that He died on the cross."

"Is that it? What about the resurrection? What about choosing not to live for yourself and to turn from your sinful life? Have you ever done that?"

"No."

I explained to him that in the book of James, it says that faith without works is dead. I shared that it isn't the works that save an individual, but it does show the changed life as you live for Christ. I read James 2:17, "'In the same way, faith by itself, if it is not accompanied by action, is dead' (NIV). You are not bearing fruit then, my brother. Would you like to receive Christ as your LORD and Savior? Are you willing to put your faith in Christ and acknowledge that He died on the cross, was buried, and three days later, he rose from the grave and ascended up to heaven?"

With his eyes filling up, he mumbled, "Yes, but I am afraid that I will lose customers if they see me praying."

"You can pray with your eyes open. God looks upon your heart. Just take a moment and call out to him and share with him what we just talked about." He smiled and said that he would. I waited next to him, praying with my eyes open out of respect to his work, and asked God to give him the strength to surrender his life to Christ. After a few moments he wiped his eyes and thanked me for sharing. He had the biggest smile possible, one that can only be displayed by someone who just received the Holy Spirit. This wasn't the same man who moments earlier was mad at God; his entire demeanor had transformed. He was calm, joyful, and at complete peace.

He offered me a hot dog and soda for free, but I wasn't hungry. He was so excited to talk to his daughter about his change. It was starting to rain harder, so I pulled my poncho out of my bag, put it on over my head, and continued down the street.

As I approached the hotel, I noticed a cab driver standing outside having a smoke, laughing at me walking in the rain with a poncho on. I went up to him and asked if he would be willing to take a picture of me, and he agreed to do so.

I introduced myself, and he told me his name was Ashour. He looked as though he was from the Middle East, with his tan skin with dark hair. He had a thick accent that also led me to believe he wasn't locally born and raised. We chatted for a moment, and then I asked him if he would share his faith with me if in return I would do the same for him. He started sharing with me that he was a Muslim. He said, "I have two angels, one on each shoulder, that keep records of everything that I do in a book. One records all of the good things, and one records all of the bad. At the end of my life, they will present the books they have kept to Allah, at which point he will decide my fate."

It was sad to hear him share that it is on one's works that someone can enter paradise. I knew this was unattainable for anyone to accomplish. "What kind of things get put on the bad list?"

With that, he asked if we could sit in his cab and continue the conversation there. There were a few other cab drivers that could overhear our discussion, and it was obvious that not all of them were happy with me asking these questions. I had no problem getting in his cab, as I wanted him to be open about his faith so that I would have the opportunity to share mine. Once in the cab, he answered my question, saying, "The things that would be written on the good side would be those I have done doing good things for others. You know, being a good person. The bad list would include anything that was displeasing to Allah. For example: smoking or lying, those would be bad."

Because he had been smoking when I approached him to take my picture, I asked, "So if smoking is bad, why do you do it?"

He smiled. "This is not good for me. I know I should not be doing it, but I like to."

"So since that is a 'bad' thing, doesn't that mean that's being written on your 'bad' list? Are you not concerned what Allah will do with that?"

"I hope that I have more good things on my list to out-weigh it." It seemed that he had the head knowledge of what he believed but not so much of the heart behind it. How could someone believe that what they were doing could be sending them to damnation? He spoke calmly with little regard for his situation.

We sat there and talked for close to two hours. I was reminded of Pastor Foglio's encouragement to be patient, and his words gave me the patience I needed as the conversation continued to go so long. As we talked, another Muslim cab driver came up to the car and started talking to Ashour about me. I was only able to make out a few words that the other man was saying, such as *Jehovah* and

Jew. He then started getting upset and began talking and then yelling at me. Ashour told him to leave, as I was in his cab so it didn't involve him. The man left and started talking to other cabbies that were nearby and pointed to where we were. I just continued with our conversation as if he had never come over.

Ashour explained to me that he would never allow his kids to smoke because he wouldn't want them to do something bad. He admitted that he was being hypocritical, but in spite of this, his children would have to obey what he said. Since I had my apologetics folder in my backpack, I pulled out a sheet I had gotten from taking a philosophy course at Liberty University with Dr. Ergun Caner that explained the differences between Islam and Christianity. As a result of some of the topics I read from that sheet, things became a little heated for a while. Topics like:

> *Salvation*:
>> Christianity—Grace alone saves: Ephesians 2:8–9
>> Islam—Good works cancel bad deeds: Surah 11:114
>
> *Forgiveness or revenge*:
>> Christianity—Jesus taught forgiveness: Matthew 5:38–39
>> Islam—Muhammad taught revenge: Surah 2:194
>
> *Crucifixion*:
>> Christianity—Jesus was crucified: 1 Corinthians 2:2
>> Islam—Jesus was not crucified: Surah 4:157

Is God love?

Christianity—God loves everyone: John 3:16

Islam—Allah is temperamental: Surah 32:13

Is God deceptive?

Christianity—God cannot lie: Titus 1:2

Islam—Allah deceives: Surah 8:30

As I shared these comparisons between what the Bible and the Quran had to say, his response was always the same: "That is not true." He didn't try to justify or even explain his reasons; it was just simple denial. His response started to soften, however, as I was able to point out the disparities in the Quran's writings. Instead of him continuing on about how this and that were not true, he started to just listen. Our conversation shifted as we talked about the horrific tragedy of 9/11. He explained to me that he didn't condone what the terrorists had done that day, as it wasn't the life that Muslims are called to live. He shared about how he and his family had since been treated differently by some people, as if they were the ones that flew the plane into the World Trade Center towers. I conveyed my deepest sympathy for the mistreatment that he and his family had experienced. I then returned the conversation back to spiritual issues and asked him if in his faith there was any way to know for sure that he would go to heaven after he died. He said, "No, Allah will decide."

I then shared with him a story I had once heard about Muhammad and his daughter coming to him near the end of his life. She asked him to pray to Allah on behalf of her salvation. Muhammad apparently told her that he wouldn't do as she asked since it is only by good works one is saved, as his own salvation was uncertain. Then I asked Ashour, "If the greatest Muslim prophet that has ever lived didn't know for sure that he would be in heaven one day, how do you not live in constant fear of Allah?"

He slumped down in his chair and put out his cigarette. "I just hope and then try not to focus on fear."

I explained to him that through Jesus, it is by His grace and not our works that one can be saved. I assured him that I had no fear of death or of hell since my security was in Christ and not good or bad lists kept by angels. I also found it interesting that it is believed the body of Muhammad was buried in a tomb in Medina but Jesus is in heaven with Allah. However, they believe Jesus was just a prophet and not deity. It is blasphemous to them to claim that Jesus was God.

I then asked what I considered to be the hardest question. "Is it true within the Muslim faith that the only sure way to be guaranteed a place in heaven is if you sacrifice your life while taking the lives of others who do not believe the same as you?"

He paused and said, "That is a cowardly way for Muslims to view life. We are called to be good and to do good. No one should take the life of someone else."

I asked him if I could pray for him, and he agreed on the condition that he could pray for me afterward. I prayed for him, and immediately following, he prayed for me. Before leaving his cab, I said, "Jesus was not a prophet. He is the Messiah. The Allah you pray to is a false god. I hope you come to see the truth over what culture and tradition has taught you. Thank you for your time, and be careful on the roads." He just looked the other way, and I got out of the car.

Though I said it kindly, I know that it was offensive to him when I said he served a false god. But the truth is, he does. From time to time, I have heard Christians say, regarding Muslims, "Well, they serve the same God we do." That is so far from the truth. Ashour believed in Jesus just as much as all devoted Muslims do. However, they view Him as a prophet and rob Him of His deity. Unfortunately, there are Christians that think all they have to do is just ask people if they believe in Jesus and that is enough to evangelize. Demons believe that Jesus is the Christ, and it is no surprise to Satan either; it doesn't mean that they are saved. I believe that we have to share that Jesus was God, give Him His deity, that He was the only one that could pay for the sins of the world through the literal crucifixion, burial for three days, and the glorious resurrection. Next, one must turn from their sins in repentance and live accordingly with the commands of Christ. Only then are we sharing the truth of Christ.

It was now almost 7:00 p.m. The rain was still coming down pretty hard, so I decided to go attempt to do my own laundry.

I know being a thirty-year-old man I should know how to wash my own clothes. But having been raised by a great mother who took care of that for me as I grew up, and now having an amazing wife that takes care of the family's laundry, I was really at a loss. After all that God had revealed to me over the last few days, I believed that I was more than capable of hand-washing my clothes in the bathroom. So, with my little box of Tide laundry soap in hand, I gathered all of my dirty clothes, and one by one, I soaked, washed, and then rinsed them out, using the combination of the sink and the bathtub Because this in and of itself was a challenge for me, I didn't know how much soap to use, so I put the whole box in. This made the rinsing out process longer than expected. Through all of the constant re-rinsing, I loved every second of it. Upon completion, I was pumped and proud of myself. Finally I was done with the rinsing out, and I was able to move on from there.

I was very excited to have clean clothes and a nice warm bed to sleep in. I hung my clothes on hangers in order to dry and then hopped into bed to get some sleep. I was going to need to get up by two thirty in the morning in order to be on time for my next bus, and I was hoping to get at least six hours of rest before I had to head out. Getting into the bed was like being hugged by a giant pile of feathers and cotton. It was as if I had forgotten what a bed felt like. I had never been so exhausted with the biggest grin on my face trying to get rest.

Getting into bed, I realized that there was a good chance my clothes wouldn't be dry by the time I had to leave. Because I love to strategize when it comes to situations like this, I got back out of bed and began making my battle plan. I grabbed my shirts from the hangers and laid them over the AC unit. I took my socks and had one cupped around the end of the hair dryer and laid it right next to the bed on "high." I took out the ironing board, plugged in the iron, and proceeded to iron my shorts on it. I had started at 7:00 p.m. with the washing process, and now it was close to ten at night; my clothes were still damp. I started laughing out loud when I thought about how smart I thought I was just a few hours before when I had this idea, to now not having a clue what to do. Not only were my clothes still wet, I apparently hadn't gotten the soap completely out of my clothes.

They had soap stains all over them, and they smelled like a box of detergent. I finally chose sleep over dry clothes, and I turned everything off and got into bed.

Getting up after a little bit more than four hours of hard sleep, I took a nice, hot shower. After putting on my damp and soap-stained clothes, I headed to the bus stop. Having the clothes on made me feel fortunate to have clothes, a shower, a bed. Even though it was slightly chilly and I smelled like a soap box, they were not dirty anymore. I had never felt like I had taken my wife's servant's heart for granted when it came to her doing my laundry, but now I was even more thankful for not only her but our washer and dryer as well.

GOD'S PLAN,
NOT MINE

Getting on the bus headed to Indianapolis, I noticed that the bus driver had a little cross pin on his vest. I asked him what his name was and if I could pray for him by name as he drove. "Fred," he said, "and that would be great." On this particular leg of my trip, there were a lot of empty seats on the bus. At four in the morning, there are not many people to talk to. I decided to maximize my time by reading another "Letter of Paul." Dr. Rob Zinn is the senior pastor at Immanuel Baptist Church in Highland, California. His letter reads:

> Ryan,
>
> As you are on your journey, remember why you're doing this. Don't let circumstances derail your desire. Look every day for what God is up to and trying to teach you. I believe you're going to learn some tremendous lessons. You are going to meet some great people and some not so great. But ask God every morning to open your eyes and your heart to let you

see what He sees. Keep the faith, brother, and remember people are not your source; God is your source.

So, "Trust in the LORD with all your heart, And do not lean on your own understanding. In all your ways (and days) acknowledge Him, And He will make your paths straight" (Proverbs 3:5–6, NASB). Also Psalm 34:4; Psalm 81:10; Matthew 9:35–38.

God Bless, be alert, and keep the faith.

In His wonderful name,

Rob Zinn

This letter seemed to put an even a stronger emphasis on me allowing God to lead as I follow in obedience. First Pastor Foglio shared from the Bible that "The steps of a good man are ordered by the LORD, and He delights in his way," and now Pastor Zinn was sharing from the Scriptures to "trust in the LORD with all your heart and do not lean on your own understanding. In all your ways (and days) acknowledge Him, and He will make your paths straight." Both of these great men provided powerful scriptures, and their meanings were being engraved into my heart. I closed my eyes and meditated over all the scriptures that had been given to me through the "Letters of Paul" I had read.

Arriving in Indianapolis, I instantly headed out of the bus depot and down the street. Passing by a Steak & Shake restaurant, I noticed an elderly man looking very upset. In talking with him, he shared that he had been kicked out of the restaurant because he did not have any money and was taking up a table for customers. "Are you hungry?" I asked.

"Yes, sir. I am."

"Come with me, and I will get you something to eat." We walked down the street a little farther and came to an Einstein's Bagel shop. I looked at him and said, "Get whatever you would like." He ordered and received his food and then walked back outside. I too went outside, and I shared with him his need for Jesus in his life. He thanked me for the food but told me he wanted to be alone. I smiled, said good-bye, and walked down the street.

I knew there were still some challenges from my "Letters of Paul" that I still hadn't done, and I was determined to get them done. However, I didn't want to force the opportunities but allow God to lead me to them. With that in mind, I came up to a man sitting on a street corner with a cup sitting before him and asking for money. He was a strong-built black man. He had a black do-rag on and was wearing a gray shirt and pants. I asked him if it would be okay if I sat with him and talked. He said he would welcome the company, and I realized that this was the person I was supposed to spend time with that Jamie Thompson had challenged me to do. Her challenge was, "I challenge you to boldly ask in Jesus's name for the opportunity to cross paths with a homeless person. Help a man, woman, or teenager along in their spiritual journey by taking the time (however long it takes) to truly hear them out, to really demonstrate that you love them because they are a child of God, and to share the good news of Jesus with them—all the while boldly asking God for their salvation."

I started by introducing myself and explained I was traveling from city to city asking people what they believed and why. He told me his name was Terry and then went on to share that he believed in Jesus. After asking him specific questions to see if he truly was born again, I was convinced that he was, as all of his answers were biblical. I asked him if he would be willing to tell me about his circumstances and how he came to be in his present situation. There wasn't even a glimpse of a smile on Terry's face as he began to share.

"When I was a young child, my father took a shotgun and killed my mother right in front of me. My brother and sister and I went to live with my grandma on my mother's side of the family. I used to get into trouble, and I was in prison for seventeen years. My sister is still in prison, and I do not know if she will ever get out." He paused for a moment and made a big sigh. "My brother is all about loose women and possessions. I woke up different times as a child and as an adult to him molesting me. The only way that I can live with him is if I accept his lifestyle and partake in it as well. I know that God doesn't want me to live that life, so I choose to live out on the streets."

Though I couldn't relate to this broken man on any personal level, I could see that my brother was hurting. "Terry, I am proud of you for staying faithful to God through all that has happened in your life. I know you have acknowledged that some things were done to you as the result of other people's choices and that some were done because of the choices you made personally. It doesn't sound like you are trying to blame God at all for your circumstances."

He looked at me and began to cry. "How do I forgive?"

"What do you mean? Forgive who?"

He wiped some of the tears from his face. "My family. All of them. I don't blame God, but I do blame them. How can I forgive?" He looked right at me with a look of desperation and complete sincerity. His face was slightly shaking.

I went from kneeling down next to him to sitting right beside him. "We forgive as Christ forgave us. It isn't an easy thing to do, but it is the only way to be in harmony with the Holy Spirit." I took my Bible and opened it to Matthew 6:14–15, where it says, "For if you forgive other people when they sin against you, your heavenly Father will also forgive you. But if you don't forgive others their sins, your Father will not forgive your sins" (NIV). I took some time and explained to Terry that when we surrender our lives to Jesus, He forgives us of all our sins. Therefore, we are called to forgive everyone for everything they do to us. I asked if I could pray for him in order that he might have the strength to forgive those who had hurt him and to give him peace for doing so.

After we prayed, Terry had a smile on his face. He shared that no one had stopped to talk to him in over a month. He went on to say that most people do not even like to make eye contact with him. As we sat there together, I watched more than thirty people pass us by, and only one looked our way, and that person only looked at me. "Terry, you have worth. You are a child of God. Though it is true that some Christians can be worthless for the cause of Christ, none are worthless to Christ." He nodded with agreement while smiling ear to ear.

I asked him if I could take a picture with him. He laughed and said, "If anyone will stop, sure." I stood up and stopped the first person closest to me and asked if he would kindly take a picture of my friend Terry and me. He agreed, took the picture, and then left quickly. I don't know if he thought we were going to ask for money, but he left faster than he had first approached us. Terry just laughed it off.

I reached in my pocket and gave Terry three dollars and change from the money I had used earlier to buy the other man his breakfast. Terry thanked me for taking the time to talk and for being concerned about him. I told him that I would be praying that he would find a good Bible church to get involved in and that he would live each day bringing glory to God. I left my new friend and headed down the street to my next church. I felt overjoyed to sit with a man who had been neglected for so long and show love and compassion to him. My entire time with him was close to thirty minutes.

I arrived at a Presbyterian church around nine in the morning. There were several children and a few women congregating in the office area. I asked one of the women if there was a pastor I might be able to speak with, and she explained that they didn't have one. They only had the day care operating at this time. I asked her where the nearest church was from there, and she directed me to a Baptist church a few blocks over.

Leaving the church, I turned and walked down the street, where I spotted an older gentleman who was out in front of his house. He made eye contact with me, so I knew that was the sign to go talk with him. I walked up and handed him a copy of the tract *Are You Innocent or Guilty?* He took it and waved me away. "I get what your point is; now leave!" I turned and continued my walk to the church. Then I heard the man yell at me, "Hey, you mean judgment day?"

I smiled and yelled back, "Yes, the only judgment that matters." He threw his hands at me as if to brush birds away. I just smiled and continued on my way.

When I arrived at the church, all the doors were locked, and there were cobwebs all over the windows and doors. I tried knocking on the front door, and then I walked around the building and tried knocking on the back door, but there was still no answer. As I stood there wondering what to do next, an overwhelming presence came over me, and I knew it was time for me to move on to the next city. If I was not received, then I would brush the dust from my feet and move on. I didn't want to be on my schedule anymore but the Holy Spirit's.

I went back to the Presbyterian church and asked if there was anyone who could drive me to the bus station. The woman I talked to said there wasn't, so I headed back out on foot again. Even though I had only been in Indianapolis for about five hours, I was at peace that I was supposed to move on. I prayed for God to send an angel or a "good Samaritan" to help me get back to the bus station in time for the next bus.

I spotted a police car and thought how perfect that would be. I waved the officer down, and he made eye contact with me but then drove away. I was kind of shocked by this, as he did not know if it was an emergency or not and at least could have given me directions back to the bus depot.

I walked down two side streets in order to get back to the main road that would lead me back into the city where the bus station was located. I turned a corner and found myself next to about fourteen Hispanic men hanging out together across the street from me. It seemed that most of them were waiting for work, but in my opinion, some of them were acting quite shady. That small group of men would huddle up close, and one would keep a lookout. I realized I had turned down the wrong street and was now lost. I noticed there was a gas station not too far down the street I was on; I would just need to go about two blocks, and I could get directions.

As I continued walking, I kept my head up and looked straight ahead. I believed that I was on a path that had been set forth by God, so by faith, I continued. Even though they were across the street, I could hear them talking, and a couple of them were discussing my backpack. I thought to myself, *It is one thing to be persecuted for your faith, but it's completely different to be jumped for any other reason.* I remember being taught that if you can run and avoid harm, then do so. Several times Jesus Himself fled harm's way. As I walked closer to the station, I just kept praying for God to be pleased with whatever might happen. If it would bring Him glory for me to get jumped, then I would rejoice in it.

Three of the men started crossing the street walking toward me, but by the time they did, I had already made it to the gas station parking lot. I asked the first person I saw pumping gas how to get back to the bus station, and they said, "I don't know; ask someone else." I went to approach the next car, which happened to have two kids and a woman inside, and as I was getting closer, she rolled up her window and drove off fast. Now there was just one car remaining, and as I went to ask for help, out stepped a man who was basically a walking mountain. He was a huge black man whom I estimated to be about six foot four and to weigh well over three hundred pounds. I said, "Excuse me, sir, but I am lost, and I am trying to find my way to the bus station. I don't have a clue where I am." He told me I could catch the city bus that had just pulled up at the curb. As I started to run to catch it, the bus pulled out, and I missed it.

Seeing what happened, he said, "Hop in. I don't really have time for this, as I am on my way to court." I thanked him and got in his car, and he peeled out. On a street with a speed limit of thirty-five miles per hour, we were peaking at fifty-five. I introduced myself, and then he explained that he was heading to court to settle a personal issue. I told him briefly how I had gone to two different churches and how neither of them had been open for business and how I needed to catch the bus that was now leaving in five minutes. We pulled up to the bus station, and I thanked him for the ride and gave him a card, telling him I would pray for him. He smiled and peeled off again. I then ran inside the bus station and was able to walk right onto the bus. I said out loud, "Thank you, Lord, for that good Samaritan."

FAITH
LIKE
BILL MAHER

This had been my first bus ride that was not either at four in the morning or very late at night, and I was excited, knowing I would more than likely have an opportunity to talk with my fellow bus riders. Sitting down in my seat, I decided I would first open and read another "Letter of Paul." This one had been written by Dr. Tom Thompson, who is the senior vice president of World Help and was Dr. David Jeremiah's executive pastor for many years. His letter read:

> A man's reach should exceed what he can grasp, or what does he need God for.
>
> —Oswald Chambers

Dear Ryan:

What an incredible journey you are undertaking. Though some may be "challenged" with this journey that God has put within your heart, no one can ever say that you failed to listen to the voice of God. That, my friend, is the most important lesson you will ever learn in life. It affects everything you touch—family, work, friends, and worship—to know that you have heard from God and that you are in partnership with what He has spoken to you about.

Ryan, there are those who, when confronted with a challenge, "act" like they have faced it, only to fall short of God's blessing. But the one who faces the challenge head on and "embraces it" is the one who has proved himself both to God and to those who will ultimately follow him ... for he will be a leader!

Paul, writing to those in Philippi, never said, "Do as I say." Rather, he wrote, "Do as I do" (4:9, NKJV). There will be some who will look at what you have accomplished and say, "I can do that." Yet, it won't be the same as what you did; it will be what they did because of you ... You can't get more thrilled than that! And only eternity will reveal who followed in your footsteps.

However, Ryan, what if *no one* did? Was it still worth it? How are you today as you read this letter? Are you stronger? Are you more in love with Jesus? Are you more passionate about your faith? Are you encouraged because of the walk of obedience you have shown to God? Then it is worth it, even if no one follows after you—because the *only* thing that matters is that you followed after Christ. It's that simple!

I can't wait to hear what God has done for you!

For your Scripture reading today, I would like for you to examine two passages and let the Spirit of God speak to you about its application. The first, I think, will be a powerful witness for what you are experiencing on this trip. The second one is a follow-up to the thirst of God within your soul. Let them both be a challenge to your thinking today. Don't just read what the words are saying. Let God speak to you as you think about what is not being said, or what is being implied, or how the players in these passages are relating to their circumstances in their day as you are today. It will challenge you, I'm sure.

2 Kings 6:8–23 and Psalm 63:1–11

As I think about a challenge for you today, I have two. First, ask God to allow you to get out of your comfort zone to share your faith with someone you would not ordinarily do that with—a specific person or group—and be bold! Second, go to the heart of the city and claim it back for God—pray for a revival to impact that town for His glory that you and your family could see in your lifetime. Like Elisha, Janice and I will be praying that God will allow you to see the supernatural things

that are hidden and that He will blind the eyes
of the enemy who may try to harm you.

> *When we obey the* LORD *in the seemingly*
> *random circumstances of life, they become*
> *pinholes through which we see the face*
> *of God. Then, when we stand face-to-*
> *face with God, we will see that through*
> *our obedience, thousands were blessed.*
> *(Oswald Chambers)*

Tom Thompson

I was encouraged by the spirit-filled words that Dr.
Thompson wrote to me. I was mindful of the fact that I
would have to approach someone that intimidated me for
the sake of LORD. I was excited for the second part of the
challenge since I never before had gone into the middle of a
city and prayed for revival of God's glory. The scripture was
like eating sweets to my soul. I was trying to hide as much as
I could within my heart.

We stopped in Dayton, Ohio, and I only had ten minutes to get off the bus and grab some food. I hadn't eaten
anything since lunch at Taco Bell the day before. With
the lack of rest, food, and water, I could tell my body was
starting to slow down. I went to the vending machine and
reached in my pocket to get some money, but all I had was
a twenty-dollar bill. There was a line of five people waiting
at the counter, so getting that twenty broken down wasn't
going to work.

I asked a young man next to me if he had change for
a twenty. He said, "No, I don't, sorry. How much do you

need?" I spotted some mini-muffins in the machine for $1.25 and said that exact amount. He reached in his pocket and gave it to me. "Here you go."

I was surprised by such generosity. "Thank you so much. At our next stop, I will make change and get it back to you."

He smiled. "Don't worry about it."

I introduced myself to him, and he told me his name was Mike. He was about six-foot-two. His glasses made him look older than I am sure he really was. When getting back on the bus, I noticed that the seats directly behind Mike were available, so I chose to sit there. Across from our rows was a young woman named Keersten, a twenty-something Caucasian with long and curly reddish hair, and the three of us started to share with one another where we were heading and why. I asked if she would take my picture so my family could see how I had traveled.

I handed them both a copy of the tract *Which One of These is Right?* Mike looked at it and, after a moment, said, "I am an Evolutionist, and I believe we made God in our image."

Keersten said, "I do not know much about evolution, but I don't think there is a God."

It was interesting that both of them didn't believe in God or even a God. She was a little passive with her response, and I could tell she was uncertain and shy about that topic. Mike, on the other hand, was very confident and sure about what it was he believed. So I said to Mike, "Can you explain to me why you believe in evolution?"

"There is no proof that a God ever existed. Man created God just like they did Santa and the Easter Bunny. There is evidence all around us that nature evolved into itself. Do you not see how man has evolved?"

"I agree; man has evolved. Not in creation or formation, but in moral and social acceptance. Things that were once either right or wrong are different today. Slavery in America is and will always be the worst thing our government ever allowed to happen. Though racism still exists in our culture today on various levels and in all races, nationally speaking, it isn't even close to what it once was." I could tell that Mike didn't like my answer because he looked away and even rolled his eyes at one point, but it was my honest opinion. I then added, "Mike, I believe you have great faith."

He looked at me with a shocked expression. "It isn't faith; it's fact."

"Just because we believe in different things doesn't mean that there isn't a level of faith involved. For example, I think Bill Maher has a great amount of faith. In fact, I admire the amount of faith he does have. I don't know exactly what he does believe in, but I do know he strongly doesn't believe what I do. Whatever he does believe, there must be a level of faith there. From my perspective, I think it requires more faith not to believe there is a God as opposed to believing there is one. So just like Bill Maher, I see you having great faith in what it is you believe."

As he sat there contemplating what I just said, I added, "There are some things that science acknowledges being in existence, but how and why they are in existence is not explained. For example, the law of gravity. My professor, Dr. Towns, would say, 'If there are laws, then there is a law-maker.' We obviously know that gravity exists, but why and how? What was here before the Big Bang took place? Or was there life before the first atom split? Science has acknowledged that the universe is finite. Since it is finite, it is hard to explain how there can be an end to something but not a beginning. How can atoms just forever be and then not again? I'm not an expert on this topic by any means. It is possible that there are those who could explain the scientific position on all of these issues and others as well. From my perspective, I would be going against logic to believe in these theories."

He started to get upset and said, "Religion is offensive and judgmental! It is as if you turn your nose down on everyone who doesn't see your view." By this time, Keersten got on her phone and was out of our conversation.

I said very calmly to Mike, "I don't know how I have judged you for anything today. I have shared with you what I believe and why. You did the same, and I admired your faith in something that has uncertainty. That is sincere."

He laughed. "I am just talking in general. You're cool, man."

We continued to talk for the remainder of the trip. He shared how he liked doing things that I would consider sinful, like smoking weed and lusting over women. He said, "It is healthy to lust." I explained how we were called to live holy lives, but by this time, I could tell that he had turned a deaf ear to me. I shared my faith and did what I believe a Christian has been commissioned to do. I casted the seed and hoped that one day it would bear fruit.

As I changed the conversation to a lighter subject like the weather, Keersten joined in again. We ended the bus ride respectfully and with no hard feelings. I thanked them for the opportunity to share with them and told them I would pray for their travel to be safe. I was now in Columbus, Ohio, and heading to my next church.

LION
CHASER

As I left the bus station, I headed to the middle of the city in order to pray, as I had been challenged by Dr. Thompson to do. With people all around me, I knelt and asked God to reclaim the city in order to bring glory to Him. After praying for a few minutes, I got up and walked to the Mt. Olivet Baptist Church.

Once in the church office, I was informed that no pastor was available, as a funeral was taking place at that time. I was told to come back by later and someone should be able to talk with me then. Since the LORD had changed my original itinerary city schedule, I continued to take all of the circumstances and situations placed before me as being what God intended. I was mindful of the challenges from my "Letters of Paul" that I still needed to complete, and turning the corner, I spotted my next challenge. Pastor McKeehan had challenged me to chase a lion, and Dr. Thompson encouraged me to be bold. Now there was a man heading in my direction that fit the bill in both categories.

I would have to say that this man was one of the most intimidating men I have ever seen. He was about six foot four and must have weighed about 260 pounds. He had a gruesome, three-inch scar over his left eye, and it looked as if he was blind from some form of knife-blade injury. He was wearing an unbuttoned flannel shirt, and as we got closer and closer, I could see his tattooed and scarred eight-pack abdomen. I went right up to him and stopped. "Excuse me, sir, will you read this for me?" I reached into my pocket and pulled out a random tract.

"What is it?"

"Truth."

He took it, and after just a few seconds of looking at it, he crumpled it into his fist, looked up at me, and yelled, "Court! I am on my way to court right now. What are you, some sort of cop?"

Apparently I had given him the tract that said *Are You Innocent or Guilty? Tips for your day in court.* I said calmly, "No, I'm not a cop. I just wanted to talk to you about Jesus." I was unsure what would happen next, but I stood my ground knowing that this was my test. I had already said the name above all names, Jesus.

While I stood there with both of my hands grabbing on to my backpack straps, the man leaned over and put his face right up to mine. Almost nose to nose, he continued to yell at me. "I am going to court, and I don't need this. *Ahhh!*"

Looking at this beast of a man in front of me clinching his hands into fists, I didn't move. I just called on the name of Jesus again. "I just wanted to share Jesus with you."

Still looking at me and repeating what he was saying, the man turned his body around and started to walk down the street. What was definitely the hand of God was that this man was still looking and talking as if I was still standing face-to-face with him. I stood there until the man had turned the corner. As he did, I let out a big sigh of relief and walked the other way.

I began praising God for delivering me from a potential beating and walked back toward the bus station in order to see what the schedule was for my bus the next day. As I was on my way, I stepped into a hotel lobby in order to get a drink of water from the drinking fountain. I stopped and talked to the three people behind the counter for a few minutes, and one of them was a young woman who expressed an interest in what I was doing. I asked, "Is it okay if I come in from time to time this afternoon just to get a drink of water?"

She said, "Sure, that is not a problem." I thanked her and continued to share why I was there and how I was going to go back to the church after the funeral was over. The young woman said, "I like the God of the New Testament, but the God of the Old Testament was kind of a jerk!" I was taken aback that she would say such a thing, but I took the opportunity to explain that, in actuality, the God of the Old and New Testaments were one in the same. She laughed it off as if it was some kind of joke. I explained to her that I needed to get going but I would be coming back soon. With that, I left the hotel and headed to the station.

NO MOVIE
TAKEN

After getting the schedule and seeing that I would have to be back at the bus station around 3:30 a.m., I left to go outside, where an attractive young woman passed by me. She couldn't have been older than twenty-one. She was talking very loudly on her cell phone and seemed to be unaware of her surroundings and those of us who were listening in. I presumed she was talking to a friend, as she said, "I'm going to have to be here for the next twelve hours because I thought my bus was going to be leaving at 5:00 p.m., but it's not leaving until 5:00 a.m."

At this moment, I noticed that there were several men—who all looked as if they were straight out of a typical "guy movie," where all of the bad guys look the same—also listening to her conversation. While still on her phone, she walked out of the bus station oblivious to all that was taking place. As she did, three men followed her out the door. I quickly walked past them and continued walking between them and the girl. I couldn't help but think of the Liam Neeson movie *Taken,* where a young pretty girl was abducted for sex trafficking. I had this overwhelming feeling that these men intended to harm her in some way.

About a half a block from the bus station, she stopped and sat down in front of an empty building. As soon as I caught up to her, I introduced myself to her as a Christian and proceeded to explain the situation to her. "I couldn't help overhearing your conversation, and I don't think you are aware of what's going on. There are men just around the corner behind us that followed you outside of the bus station, and I wanted you to be aware of that and ask you if I might stand just a few feet away from you in order to make sure you are okay."

A frightened look came over her. "Oh my gosh, I didn't even know. What are you, some kind of pastor or something?"

I smiled. "No, just a Christian who wants to make sure you are okay."

She stood up and looked around the corner at the men standing there. "I am going to get a ride to my friend's house." She told me her name was Morgan, and then she called her friend. The two of them agreed that the best thing for her to do was to get a cab in order for her to get to her friend's house.

As I was sharing with her why I was there, a cab driver pulled up and rolled down his window. "Hey, pretty lady, need a ride?"

She looked at me and asked, "Should I go with him?"

"Morgan, it's your choice. If you think it's okay, then make your decision."

She looked at the cab driver again. "Okay."

I quickly gave her a business card. "Please call my office and tell them you got to your friend's house okay. I will not get the message until I get back home, but if for any reason I don't get that call, I will come back here looking for you."

She took my card, smiled, and said, "Okay."

I went to the cab driver and said, "Give me all of your information. I want to make sure she gets there safely, and if she doesn't, I will come looking for you."

With a surprised look on his face that was almost offended, he said, "Okay. What is this all about? Is she your girlfriend?"

She and I both smiled, and I said, "No, she is my sister." I whispered, "In Christ." Not having the time to see if she was a Christian or not at that time, I wanted to show her a brother's love through Christ.

He gave me all of his information, and I said to her, "Talk to you later."

"Thanks, brother." She smiled at me as they drove away. I prayed and asked God to give her safe travel as she went to her friend's home as well as her bus trip the next day. I started to walk back to the church in hopes that the funeral would now be over and that I would be able to talk with a pastor.

Arriving at the church and again entering the office reception area, I saw that there were now fewer people, and I was hoping I hadn't lost the opportunity to speak with a pastor. After I asked the receptionist at the front desk if there was a pastor available, she left her desk in an effort to find out. When she returned, she came back with another woman who introduced herself as Reverend Deborah. "How can I help you?"

I took a few minutes and explained to her, as I had done with the other pastors at the previous churches, what I was doing there and what I was hoping the church could do to assist me. She encouraged me to go home.

She said, "You need to go home and be a husband and father through Christ. Live out the faith that you have obtained in your household." I didn't quite know how to take this counsel. Was it coming from a woman's perspective or from the Holy Spirit? Would I listen better if she was a man? I calmed my emotions of uncertainty by asking God for wisdom. James 1:5–6 tells us to ask for wisdom in complete faith. I waited patiently for peace about the advice I was being given as she continue to share. After that, she made a phone call to the local YMCA, but no one answered. She said she was aware of another shelter in the area, but when I informed her of when I would need to be back at the bus station, she knew that I wouldn't be able to make it if I stayed there. Unfortunately, that was all that church was able to do for me at that time. I realized the timing was difficult with the funeral that had just taken place.

Deborah prayed over me and asked God to give me safe travels as I journeyed back home. She was a very kind and encouraging woman of God. I thanked her for her time and headed back toward the hotel in order to get another drink of water.

A WELCOME INVITATION
TURNS TO
THREATEN LIFE

I walked back into the hotel and greeted the same young woman I had talked with before. She was a young twenty-something with long black hair and glasses. She always was smiling to everyone she had a conversation with. She asked, "What did the church say?"

"They were unable to help."

She looked at the clock on the wall. "I am off at 6:00 p.m. If you like, you are welcome to come with me to my brother's house for a barbecue."

Since I didn't have any accommodations for the evening, I accepted the offer as a special opportunity from the LORD. "That would be great. Thank you."

Since I had a little time to burn until six, I walked back outside and talked to a few other people within the hotel area. No real opportunity to share my faith presented itself, and before I knew it, it was six. I went to the hotel parking lot, where she was already in her car. She pulled up, and I got in and said, "This is very kind of you. I know my wife will be happy to know that I was able to enjoy at least one home-cooked meal while I was on my trip."

Even though I had my wedding ring on my left ring finger and had shared with her in an earlier conversation that I was very happily married, I felt that it was important to again acknowledge that I was a married man. As we were on our way, I asked, "By any chance, are there any cats at the house?"

"Yes, why?"

I explained to her that I was greatly allergic to cats. "Would it be okay with you and your family if I just hung out in the backyard?"

Though she expressed that she felt terrible, she was very gracious and said, "Absolutely, not a problem."

As we were driving, she explained to me that she, her two brothers, and her oldest brother's girlfriend were all Jehovah's Witnesses, though none of them were practicing members any longer. She went on to tell me that about ten years before, her oldest brother had actually been a missionary overseas for a few years. She didn't share why they no longer practiced that belief, but it didn't seem as though she cared to go back. Before we arrived at the house, the picture became more and more clear as to how I thought the evening might go and what God had in mind. I would be miles away from the bus station, confined to a stranger's backyard, surrounded by people of different faith. I was excited.

When we arrived at the house, I was greeted by the oldest brother and his girlfriend. The two girls and I walked down the street to the store to pick up some more things that were needed for dinner. Once there, we were met by her other brother and his friend. We talked about general life topics such as schooling, weather, and places people had traveled to. They finished their shopping, and we returned to the house.

The weather started to change, and it began to sprinkle. They left me outside by myself for a short time. I didn't feel out of place even a bit, and I tried to be a good guest, even though I was not eating their food or going into their house. I still did not have much of an appetite, even though I had very little to eat this entire trip so far. Food wasn't as important to me as looking for opportunities to share. I was just so grateful, as these were the first people to open their home to me. The two girls came back outside and asked what my favorite part of my trip had been so far. Before I could answer them, they offered me a cigarette as they each lit a cigarette for themselves. The only smoking I had ever done was one time when I was eighteen, and that was with a Swisher Sweet Blunt (cigar). I hated it. I told them I didn't smoke and proceeded to answer their question.

"I have really enjoyed meeting people of all walks of life, just like yourselves. Having met so many different people and hearing their life stories has really helped me grow in my faith. Seeing how God has led me from place to place has given me clarity and peace with me being out on the road."

One of the girls asked, "Why are you doing it?" She was surprised that I would leave my family and the comforts of home. She was a petite young lady and must have had at least ten years between her and the oldest brother.

I smiled. "I wanted answers to my limits. I believe in something greater than myself. However, I felt like I was being suffocated by my own limitations. I wanted and needed to grow beyond what my daily routine and surroundings offered me."

"I could never do something like that. I would be too scared."

"I was very scared when I first started my trip. In fact, I cried and tried quitting. If I wasn't doing this for a greater purpose, then I never would have taken that first step of faith in the first place."

Knowing about their upbringing was a great advantage as I shared with them the reasons they should step out of any form of traditionalism and serve the LORD by faith. "I have attended church my whole life. My father was a pastor for over twenty-five years, and so, growing up, I was always at church. Now as an adult sitting in church each week, I decided that for me, there was a huge part of being a Christian that I wasn't practicing. As I focused on the Great Commission, I realized that the command from God was the 'go tell' message and not the 'come hear' message. I believe that church services should place more emphasis on teaching about having a relationship with Christ instead of just entertaining members with theology." They seemed to listen to everything I was sharing and could definitely see genuine interest in what I believed.

As I was sharing, the younger brother came out and called both of them back into the house. There I was again, outside by myself but not alone. I prayed, "God, please allow me the opportunity tonight to share Your Word and proclaim Your truth. Please give me the words and the courage to be bold in this place. Thank you for the cross and the sacrifice you made. I love you, and I again give my all to you. Amen."

A few minutes later, the rain stopped, and everybody that was in the house came outside where I had been waiting. The friend of the younger brother was a strong Agnostic and was drinking more and more as the night went on. He was a Caucasian man with tattoos all over his arms. He was balding at an early age, but I believed him to be in his late twenties. He wore dark gray glasses. For close to five hours, I listened to them as they blasphemed God, drank, and smoked. This was by far the most I had been out of my comfort zone during my trip. Even though this was the environment I found myself in, this family really did show love to one another as well as to me. They were respectful to me, and I could tell by the way they acted and communicated with one another that they deeply loved one another.

Almost at 11:30 p.m., I asked if they would all sit down and allow me to share what I believed with them. The friend was hesitant, but the oldest brother took the lead by sitting first. They seemed to be willing to listen to whatever I was going to talk about. As they all took their seats, I took a deep breath and then began to do "open air preaching" for the first time since I had left home on my trip. I began sharing how sin had separated us from God. I explained that it was only through the finished work of the cross of Christ that one could be saved. At this point, the friend had heard enough.

"Are you saying that I have to accept your belief? Huh? Because if that is what you are saying, I am not going to listen to that! We won't be cool!"

I said calmly, "I am saying that, according to what the Bible teaches, apart from receiving Jesus as your LORD and Savior, no one can be in heaven with God."

I continued my preaching, even when he stood up and said, "If you keep talking, I am going to mess you up!" I could see the rage building up, as one fist was already clinched and he was leaning forward in his seat.

In spite of his threats, I continued sharing the truth. When he took a step toward me, the oldest brother stood up and said, "Sit down! Let him finish." The brother put his hand on the friend's chest and stood between us. He seemed to naturally be protective of those in need or in harm.

I finished about five minutes later and asked if anyone had any questions. The younger brother seemed very knowledgeable about different world religions, and he had adapted a personal philosophy that focused on love being the thing that really mattered. I did my best to answer specific questions they asked, but I encouraged them not to hold on to previous knowledge they may have had about receiving Christ. I knew before I had even spoken that, as Jehovah's Witnesses, their understanding of Jesus was different from what I would be sharing.

The two young women offered to give me a ride back to the bus station, so I said my good-byes and thanked them for the invitation to join them for dinner. Each of them wished me well, including the one guy who had gotten so upset with what I was sharing, albeit after he had calmed down. I thanked them again for their hospitality and for demonstrating genuine love for one another. As I was leaving, the oldest brother called me over and gave me a hug. He whispered in my ear, "Be safe."

"Thank you for allowing me to speak and be a guest at your house. I encourage you to get close to Christ. There was a time in your life when you dedicated yourself to missionary service. Though I don't, it seems that you yourself no longer agree with that religion today. In spite of this, I still believe you have a heart that could bring glory to God. Seek Him, believe, and receive Him." He smiled and went inside the house. The two girls drove me back to the station, and I thanked them both for their servants' hearts.

I believe having been threatened earlier in the day had given me the courage to stand when it happened again. I couldn't help but think about young David and how, when asked by King Saul why he thought he could defeat the giant, Goliath, when none of the other soldiers in his army had been willing to do so, David took that opportunity to explain to Saul that on two different occasions while he was attending his father's sheep, once a bear and then, another time, a lion had come. He went on to tell him how God had delivered both into his hands, and it was those experiences that had given him the confidence and the faith in God's ability to deliver him. That gave him the courage to step out into battle. I could feel the armor of God upon me. I was ready for anything. I was also extremely tired. I sat down on a bus station bench, and soon after, I fell asleep.

TWO-HOUR
CITY

"Help! Please! Someone come quick!" The voice was that of a woman yelling in the bus station. Waking up startled from the deepest of sleeps, I put my glasses on to see that a large man had collapsed on the floor about fifteen feet away from me. There were about half a dozen people already standing around by the time I got there, and one was equipped with medical gear. After a few minutes, the man was revived and sitting up and talking. Apparently he had fallen asleep on one of the benches and fallen, hitting his head on the ground. He was given some water, and two of the people sat next to him in order to make sure he was okay until an ambulance arrived. I heard someone say, "That's how fast it can go. Life is here and then it can be gone."

It was a true statement. Apart from suicide, no one knows for sure when they will take their last breath, and that was a sobering reminder to me to keep talking to people about Jesus. Even though I had only gotten a total of seven hours of sleep over the previous three days, I was on a mission, and there was still work to be done.

My bus had now pulled up, so I gathered my things and proceeded to board. As I got on the bus, I looked for anyone who was awake that I might talk to, but each person in his or her seat was sound asleep. Since there was no one for me to talk to on the bus, I spent the entire bus ride talking to God.

When I arrived in Cincinnati, Ohio, I felt a strong impression from the LORD that I needed to go on to Lexington, Kentucky, on the next available bus. In order for that to happen, I would need to wait for two hours. Since I had some time, I spent it talking to other people who were also waiting in the station. The majority of my time was spent talking to a Christian married couple that was waiting in the station with their three children.

As we talked, they became very transparent and shared with me that they were having some problems raising their children. They told me that they weren't involved in a local church at the moment and, in truth, weren't really big fans of going to church at all. They claimed they hadn't found a church in which they had really felt welcomed. I encouraged them to keep looking, as the Bible teaches that as Christians, we are to be in fellowship with one another. I shared that you cannot love the LORD and hate His church. Though they both were saved, in talking with them, I could tell that they were still fairly young in their faith.

During our conversation, one of their children disobeyed their instructions two times for the same thing, and each parent handled the situation differently. I suggested they be patient and consistent when it came to disciplining their children. I shared that I was not an expert on this subject, but these were things that my wife and I practiced that, for us, seemed to make the issue of obedience and our children an easier process. Though the young children can be trying at times, each child is a precious gift. As they thanked me for taking the time to talk with them, I noticed the line for my bus was forming, so I said good-bye and took my place in line.

Not everyone I tried to talk to while standing there was responsive, but I noticed that those who did all had something to share. This entire trip was helping me to learn the importance of loving my neighbor more and more. For me, this was significant, as prior to this trip it hadn't come naturally to me to talk to other people about prayer requests. I was learning that the more I did it, the easier it was becoming.

I sat on the bus with a seat open next to me. Across the way sat a young, dark-haired man by himself, so I introduced myself and asked where he was going. He told me his name was Tom, and he said, "I am going to enlist in the army."

I thought that was great. "No greater love than to lay down your life for another. Your act of service and willingness to place yourself in harm's way for others reminds me of another man that was willing to sacrifice His life for others as well." I went on and explained why it was necessary for Jesus to die but that he had done so willingly and freely from a heart of love. Jesus laid down his life; no one took it from Him. "Why are you enlisting?"

He shocked me by saying, "I want to die." He shared that his life was full of pain and that the things that brought him any kind of joy were strippers, getting drunk, and just being wild. I felt sad as I heard him admit that he felt so empty each time after he had indulged in one of these areas. He went on to say that oftentimes he would try to do adrenaline-junkie activities in order just to feel alive.

I was thrilled to be able to share with him. "Jesus came into the world in order to give new life and to give it more abundantly. It seems you lack purpose and that you are hoping to find it in the army. May I pray with you?"

"Okay." He sat very still, almost motionless, as if he wanted to soak up everything that I had to say. As I prayed for him, I thanked God for salvation and explained clearly what that meant. Afterward, he asked me if he could just sit in silence for a while, and we didn't talk from that point on.

VBS
AND
PATCH

I arrived at the Lexington station excited to see what God had for me on this, the last leg of my trip. Now beginning my fifth day, I had more or less lowered my expectations as it related to any help I might receive from a church, but in spite of that, I was ready and willing for whatever the LORD had for me that day. I opened up my last "Letter of Paul." This one had been written by Dr. Ed Hindson. Dr. Hindson is the assistant chancellor and dean of the Institute of Biblical Studies at Liberty University in Lynchburg, Virginia. In his letter he wrote:

> Ryan,
>
> My prayers will be with you on your Faith Walk journey. Remember, there are many "mountains" to climb and "valleys" to cross on life's journey. David also realized this when he wrote: "The steps of a good man are ordered by the LORD; He delights in his way" (Psalm

37:23 NKJV). Let God direct your steps, and you will find unexpected "treasures" of blessing along the way. Remember, your wife and children are waiting at the final destination when you return home—waiting to hear of your journey and share in its reward.

Dr. Ed Hindson

What a perfect last letter for my trip. The overwhelming theme of allowing God to direct my steps was seen in the fact that I was in Lexington two days earlier than I had originally planned.

I headed toward the church, and on my way there, I could see that there were several strip clubs in the neighborhood. At that moment, I had the idea of standing outside and preaching at one of them later that night, but first I wanted to see what else God might have for me that day. I arrived at the Consolidated Baptist Church, and when I walked inside, I could see a number of small children playing. It was Vacation Bible School week, and it reminded me that my wife was teaching a VBS class at our church back home while I was away.

Once I got to the front desk, I asked if there was a pastor available to speak with. I was told that someone would be able to speak with me within the next couple of hours. I asked if I might leave my bag in their office until I came back, and I was told that I could. I wanted to wait and ask someone in leadership about accommodations for the night. With my load now lightened, I headed back toward the part of town where I had first arrived in the city. I spotted a shopping center that had a Walmart and thought that would be a great place to interact with a lot of people. The walk from the bus to the church was about a mile, and my walk from the church to the Walmart was about the same.

As soon as I arrived at the parking lot, I started handing out my gospel tracts to the people coming and going in and out of the store. I noticed some employees on a break sitting outside at a table, so I went over and gave each of them a tract. As I did, one employee told me that I needed to go into the store and speak with a manager about handing out materials while on store property. So I went into the store and inquired about with whom I should talk regarding getting permission for passing out my tracts. I waited for about fifteen minutes, and then one of the store managers came and spoke to me. "Here is a form that needs to be filled out prior to your being able to hand out materials on Walmart property. However, you cannot hand out anything today, and your paperwork must be approved before you can proceed."

I explained, "I'm only here for the day, and I'm not selling anything. If I just stand there with my handout, would that be okay? I will not talk unless someone talks to me first."

Standing straight up and looking me right in my eyes with no emotion, she said, "No. I am sorry, but that is not our policy."

"I understand. Thank you for your time, and I will not hand anymore cards out to people on your property."

I was a little disappointed because I viewed the possibility of being able to share with a lot of people without having to walk so much. As I left the store, I spotted a Mexican restaurant called Taco Tico. I hadn't yet eaten anything, so I hurried into the restaurant and ended up talking to Rick, whom I think was the owner or manager. Having never been there, I asked him for his opinion as to what he thought was the best thing to eat on the menu. He offered his opinion, and I ordered my food. While I was waiting at the counter, he said, "So where are you from?"

I told him I was from Tennessee, and then I shared what I was doing on my trip.

He responded by saying, "I admire what you are doing."

When my food came, he asked if I would like to have some of their Cinnamon Crustos, which were deep-fried corn tortilla wedges covered with cinnamon and sugar. I answered enthusiastically, "Sure, that would be great." He then handed me two bags absolutely free of charge. I thanked him for his generous gift and ate my meal. The food I had ordered was good, but the Cinnamon Crustos were great! I ended up thanking Rick several times for the tasty dessert, and I asked him if there was anything I could pray for him about.

"It was my pleasure. If you could pray for my mother, that would be great. It is personal, but I would appreciate it." As I left, I told him I would be praying for him. I walked out of the restaurant with a full stomach and ready to give the street another chance. I was brushed off by three consecutive people and found myself close to the church again. I decided to see if there might be someone available now.

After I walked inside, I was introduced to a woman named LaTonya, who was overseeing the VBS program. She was a larger young black woman with a great big smile. I could tell she loved the Lord and the children. I asked if we could go somewhere and talk for a few minutes, and she agreed. She took me to the conference room, and after inviting me to sit down, she went and checked to see if someone else might be available to join us as well. When she came back, she introduced me to a new staff member by the name of Roy, who had just been hired a few days prior to my showing up. He was an average-set Caucasian man with glasses and a buzzed head. As the two of them sat down around the table with me, they allowed me to share my needs.

While we were talking, I remembered that I hadn't yet completed the challenge that Pastor McKeehan had given me regarding singing. I asked them if they would be willing to let me sing to them, and in return, they would provide me with some money that I would in turn use to buy a homeless person some food and then share the gospel with them while they ate. To my great joy, they smiled and agreed to my proposition. Now, I'm not a singer, and I knew that this would be a very embarrassing and humbling moment for me. I closed my eyes, took a deep breath, and just pictured Jesus smiling as I began to sing. I sang a song about bringing glory to the King. When I was through singing, I looked at my audience of two and said, "Thank you for being willing to listen to that."

They were both very kind, and being true to his word, Roy gave me five dollars. LaTonya excused herself and went to see if the senior pastor was on campus. A few minutes later, she returned with the pastor. The senior pastor, not knowing very much about why I was there or what I was doing, had graciously stepped out of a meeting to pray and lay hands on me. Upon completing his prayer on my behalf, I thanked him for his time, and he went back to his meeting.

Both Roy and LaTonya volunteered suggestions regarding places I might be able to stay. They were describing several different centers for people who were in need of a cot for the night. I explained that, unless one of these centers would make an exception and allow me to leave earlier than most policies would allow, I would be unable to catch my bus the next morning. Roy called a place called the Hope Center but was informed that I wouldn't be able to stay there. Roy wrote down his cell phone number on a piece of paper as well as the number to the Hope Center in the hope that something might change. I thanked him for his efforts. LaTonya then invited me to go with her to get some lunch.

"Our church has a weekly ministry on Wednesdays where we provide meals for people in our community, so there will be people you can talk to," she said. Even though I was not hungry as a result of the delicious Crustos I had recently eaten, I was excited to learn that a church was not only willing to feed me but people in their community as well. I followed her into the cafeteria area, where there were about fifteen to twenty people sitting and eating. As I looked over the room, I noticed two men that were sitting at the end of one of the tables, and I decided I would go sit with them. One man had long, straight brown hair with a thick mustache. The other man was in his sixties, Caucasian, and had long blondish/white hair with a long beard to match. Most of his hair was coming out under from his black cowboy hat. They seemed to be more social than the other people at the tables.

I introduced myself to the two men, and they told me that their names were Joe (the mustache) and Patch (the cowboy hat). They told me they had been friends for some time, and at present, Patch was living with Joe. Patch was rather quiet as he was eating his food, but Joe was willing to engage in a conversation about Christ. I asked him if he would be willing to take a look at the tract inscribed with *Which One of These Is Right?*.

He put his fork down and read over the entire card. He seemed open to reading whatever it was I handed him with no reservation. After reading it, he said, "All of them are right except the Jehovah's Witnesses." As I went over the differences of these religions with him, I made the distinction that though it was true that Catholicism and Christianity have some similarities, in a lot of their practices, they are very different. He was surprised to find out that there were so many differences between religions. He assumed for the most part they believed the same thing.

After I explained the importance of having a personal relationship with Jesus, Patch shared that he was a Christian. He also said, "I have been homeless for over twenty-eight years, and I love it. I know where to get hot meals throughout the week, and there is even a place that will do my laundry for me. Joe and I like to fish, and as far as I am concerned, it is all I need."

I found it interesting that Patch was so willing to openly acknowledge that he freely chooses to be homeless. Though I would have to say that of the people I had met on my trip in similar situations, none of them were happy about being homeless. Patch, on the other hand, seemed to relish the fact that he was homeless and was living his life seemingly with great joy. He told me that he played the guitar and had written a song about Jesus. I told them if the two of them would start coming to the church and attending the services, I would tell LaTonya about Patch's song and encourage her to have them sing to the children. He was so excited about that possibility that he couldn't stop smiling.

We headed outside to get Patch's guitar, and to my surprise, it was in Joe's car. I never thought of a homeless person having a car. My perception had certainly changed from stereotyping all homeless people. Patch grabbed his guitar out of the car and began to play and sing his song.

As he sang, it was really very moving, because I could tell that he had written it from a painful past. When he finished the song, I thanked him and then turned and asked Joe if he had thought about what we had talked about earlier.

He said, "I know what you're saying is truth."

So I challenged him. "Then why not get involved here at the church and start living that life of faith and service?" He looked as though he was deep in thought and really considering coming to the church.

We shook hands, and I headed back down the street again in order to continue my witnessing. As I got down to the end of the church's driveway, I heard a car horn honk. As I turned to look, I saw it was Joe and Patch, and they were driving toward me. They pulled up and said, "Hop on in. We'll give you a ride."

"Sweet, thanks."

They asked me where I wanted to go, and I asked if they could drop me off back at the bus station area, as I wanted to stand and preach outside some of the strip clubs. So that is where they dropped me off. They both admired my zealousness to share the gospel and my boldness to do it wherever.

Walking around the first building, I read a sign that read "No loitering." After having been through what I had with Walmart, I knew I would be breaking the law, and I couldn't in good conscience knowingly break the law while at the same time asking God to bless my efforts. As much as I wanted to stay and provide a much-needed alternative message to the men coming to visit these establishments, I decided instead to walk on back to the bus station and see who the LORD would have there waiting for me to talk to.

A TWISTED
MIND

As I was on my way back to the station, what I had read in Dr. Hindson's letter kept repeating in my head. "Remember, your wife and children are waiting at the final destination when you return home, waiting to hear of your journey and share in its reward." At that very moment, a wave of peace came over me to go home. God spoke to my heart, and I felt a calm assurance that I had accomplished what I had set out to do. Now the time had come for me to take what I had learned and start applying it to every area of my life. I walked in and got my last bus ticket, which would take me back to Knoxville. As I went over to sit down on a bench in the station, a man walked in. He was wearing some dark homely clothes and was not well kept up, and from where I was sitting, it seemed he was very disturbed.

He had a small radio around his neck that had a leather strap attached to it. He sat down near to me and then started talking to himself. As he sat there, he tried to adjust the signal but was not able to receive anything clearly. Though he kept trying, the radio would make a loud screeching sound, causing him to become angry, which led him to aggressively bite at his strap.

The room we were in was very small, and the other two people waiting for their bus now seemed to get nervous. One of them actually got up and walked outside, which now just left me and one other woman. We had briefly talked earlier, and she had shared with me that she was a Christian. She had shown me a picture of some clouds that she had taken a month prior that looked like angel wings. She admitted that she knew the clouds were not really an angel but had been moved by the image because the cloud looked so beautiful.

As the man with the radio finally calmed down for a moment, I could see the woman take a huge sigh of relief. Then, suddenly, the man stood up and screeched again and started biting his strap. He began pointing at the wall in front of him and muttering some words I was unable to decipher. He then turned and walked toward the woman. She grabbed on to the handles of the chair she was sitting on and became frozen. As he continued walking toward her, I stood up, standing between the two of them. The man stopped and started pointing his finger at me in a threatening way and biting that leather strap. I began to pray out loud for God to give him peace and a clear mind. This made the man even angrier with me, but it also caused him to leave and walk outside.

The woman was very thankful and admitted to me that she was terrified. While we waited together for our bus to arrive, the man with the radio never came back in. Once our bus did arrive, we stood in line to get on, and as we did, up walked the same man. Sure enough, he got in the same line and was getting on the same bus with us. I let the woman go ahead of me. She went several rows back and sat next to the window and put her bag on the aisle seat next to her. I sat down on the seat across from her, and she looked at me with a reassured smile. The man did get on the bus and sat about four rows in front of us. He seemed to have calmed down, and though I wouldn't say he was acting like everyone else on the bus, he was no longer attacking himself or making such violent gestures and noises. He sat down in his seat with just some slight movement but did not make a sound.

A young Hispanic girl was sitting next to me, and she didn't speak any English. On the bus ride back to Knoxville, we had to make a routine stop. At this particular stop, we had the opportunity of getting something to eat at a Burger King restaurant. I tried to help the young girl, but due to our language barrier, she didn't understand what I was saying. She then had a brilliant idea and took her cell phone and called her dad, as he spoke English fluently. She then handed me the phone. I would speak with him and then hand the phone to her, and her dad would share with her what I had said. She handed me money, and her father told me what she wanted, so I had her stay on the bus while I ran and got her food.

When I got back on the bus, I gave her the food and went to sit down when someone tapped me on my shoulder. I turned around, and it was the man from the station.

"Can I have a dollar for a soda?"

It was remarkable. It was as if it were a completely different person. "Of course. Because it is raining, would you like me to go get it for you?"

"No, that is okay."

I gave him the dollar, and he went and got his drink. The woman who sat across from me looked at me with big eyes and said, "Wow."

Everyone got back on the bus, and we were headed to my last stop. I decided to go big, so I stood up and walked down the entirely full bus and handed each person a tract. "Please read this, and if you have any questions or thoughts, please let me know." Before I sat down, I went up to a soldier that was wearing his military uniform and said, "Sir, on behalf of me and my family, I want to thank you for your service. We have a deep appreciation for those who serve in our armed forces."

He didn't smile. In fact, he almost cried. "Thank you. It has been difficult, and I haven't been given much support for my duty. Thank you."

I put my hand on his shoulder. "The least all of us can do is say thank you." I squeezed my hand, smiled, and went back to my seat.

I could overhear people discussing the issues on the tracts as we were getting closer to the station. Before stepping off of the bus, I found a man that spoke both English and Spanish to help the young lady get to her destination. I grabbed my bag and touched down in Knoxville.

The church where my wife was working VBS was over four miles away from the station. I decided I would make the walk and finish strong. Even though Magnolia, the street I would have to take, is where one could find prostitution, drugs, and gangs with the occasional drive-by, I knew that God had brought me through the fire; I could handle one of the worst parts of town.

THE PATH
HOME

Starting my walk down the street toward home, I remembered that I hadn't completed the challenge by Pastor McKeehan. I earned the money by singing to Roy and LaTonya earlier that day, but I hadn't used it to pay for the meal of a homeless person and then share Jesus with them while they ate. I talked to God the entire walk back and started to reflect on all of the people and lessons He'd brought forth to me. I don't have a natural smile, but I know that I was grinning from ear to ear the entire time I was walking. It wasn't because I was going to see my family or share my journey with them, but it was having complete confidence in my faith with God and having peace that can only come from Him.

As I was walking, I came up to a KFC. Sitting outside was a man that appeared not to have eaten for some time. He was an old black man with a wiry gray beard and hair that was untamed. I asked him if I could buy him a meal and if he would allow me to share the truth of Jesus with him. He was all for it, though I couldn't tell you if he wanted to hear what

I wanted to say or not. He gave me his order, and I walked inside and got everything he asked for. I came outside with his food and drink, and we sat on a public bench together. His name was Bobby, and while he ate, I shared.

About halfway through our conversation, a car with tinted windows, large rims, and loud rap music playing pulled up. The passenger window rolled down, and a large man yelled, "Hey, yo, Bobby. You okay?"

I could see that the car was full and all eyes were on me. Bobby didn't respond to the man. I said, "I just wanted to make sure Bobby got something to eat and talk to him about Jesus."

The man looked right at me. "Well, I guess there is nothing wrong with that." The man gave a signal to the driver, and the window rolled back up as they drove away.

Bobby, having to be closer to seventy than to sixty, acknowledged that he had Jesus inside of him. He shared that he had drifted away from the LORD for some time but that He was always with him. I encouraged him to get back to the place where his life reflected the love of Christ. I invited him to attend my church, and I prayed with him and then headed back on the path.

The time was getting later, and as the darkness came, so did more people on the street. I prayed, asking God to purify the city and to reclaim it back to Himself as I had in Columbus. I prayed that if He found any wickedness to convict the person and for repentance to come.

As I prayed for purification, it began to rain. Not only did it rain, but it rained extremely hard. Wind blew by so fast that one gust almost knocked me off my feet. As I ducked under a tree to grab my poncho, I realized that there was nobody else left on the street. The LORD was providing for me a safe passage home. I continued down the road, and as my prayer intensified, so did the weather. Purification and conviction was the theme of my prayer. As I asked for each individual to be not only held to accountability but also convicted of any past or present sin that they have committed, a piece of hail landed right next to me.

It was the middle of June in Knoxville without a cloud in the sky when I left the station, and now it was hailing. Amazed at what was taking place around me, I continued to call out to God. This was a completely different prayer than that of the one I had in Chattanooga that was consumed with doubt and fear. This was a prayer of both confidence and boldness. Then, in midsentence, a large piece of hail hit me on my head. I continued on praying, and as soon as I asked for conviction again, two pieces of hail hit me on the head, almost knocking me over.

I realized that I too still had unconfessed sin in my own life. Though my faith had grown tremendously, I was being humbled by ice so that I wouldn't become self-righteous. My prayer changed, and every possible wrong thing that I had ever done that came to mind, I made right with the LORD. In order for me to have a clear conscience, I needed to make right everything, regardless of how big or small I made them to be. It was still sin, and I didn't want a trace of it within me.

As my prayer changed, the hail ceased. By the time I was done praying, the rain had almost come to a complete stop. As I sang my theme chorus out loud as I walked, "I have decided to follow Jesus, though none go with me, I still will follow, the world behind me, His cross before me, no turning back, no turning back," the rain stopped.

I could see the cross on top of the church, and I knew I was almost there. When I arrived at the church, there were only a handful of clouds left in the sky. I marveled at the wondrous power God has over the weather. I walked into where my wife's classroom was, and I knocked on the door. Mrs. McKeehan, Pastor Mark's wife, answered the door. She was surprised to see me. "What are you doing here? Is everything okay?

"I am great. The LORD told me to come home. Is Shannan here?"

"No, Jack is sick, so she isn't here."

"Please don't call her. I will walk home. Thanks." I live less than five minutes away, so I walked on over and knocked on the door, but there was no answer. I went over to my sister's, and I was greeted with a big hug. "Shannan and the boys are at Mom and Dad's."

Now, that was about twenty miles away, and I didn't feel like making that walk. I used my sister's phone and dialed my wife's cell. She answered, "Hey."

I said very tiredly, "Hi, honey."

She began to cry with excitement. "Where are you? Are you okay?"

"I am home. Come home with the boys, please."

She said with joy, "We are leaving now!"

Because I was exhausted from my trip and it now was the third day without a shower, my sister let me into my place. I had about thirty minutes to get cleaned up before my family arrived, so I got into the shower. I thanked God for my shower, roof, bed, and AC unit—everything that I came into contact with. I realized that I had prayed and thanked God before for those things, but I never did it with a heart that was filled with pure gratitude. While I was in the shower, I started laughing about how I didn't have to dry off with brown paper towels. However, I was mindful of what that meant to me while I was out on the road.

By the time I got out and got dressed in some fresh, non-soap-stained clothes, I heard the car pull up. I went to the front door and stood about five feet into the house. I could hear my wife running up to the door. The door opened, and there was my beautiful wife with Parker in her hands and Jackson right next to her. With a huge smile and watery eyes, she embraced me. I hugged all three of them at once. My heart cried out with overwhelming joy to God for bringing me the greatest gifts that he had given me back into my arms. My three-year-old son looked up at me and asked, "Daddy, can I go with you next time?"

I knelt down and picked him up. "Son, I would love for you to come with me to tell people about Jesus. That would be the greatest day you and I could have." He smiled, and I kissed his cheeks at least a hundred times. I held Parker and felt that within five days he'd grown twice the size. Unless an opportunity was presented for me to go away, I never wanted to miss another day of their lives.

My wife and I put Parker to bed, and I did our normal routine with Jackson: We each take time to pray and thank God. Then we recite John 3:16 and sing "Jesus Loves Me." I really missed that time with him. Once Jackson was asleep, my wife handed me five papers. I didn't know what they were, but I could see that they were very important to her. I sat down to read.

BEYOND
FAITH

I began to read a journal that my wife had made about what she was feeling and going through while I was gone. She shared things that were fun and informative, like Jackson going poo-poo in the potty every day. However, she shared that she had a very difficult time saying good-bye to me.

Without me knowing, she chose to fast while I was on my trip. Every time she would get hungry, she would pray for me. Every time she missed me, she would pray for me. She wrote, "I know this week will be the most I have ever prayed or trusted God in my life." I didn't realize the impact of my choice to go find that surviving faith would also have an effect on my wife's faith. She knew that I was hurt in Chattanooga and that I struggled to continue on my journey, but she continued to pray and trust.

On Sunday, while I was in Nashville, she wrote, "I pray you get strength today from Him to continue on and finish what you started. Your boys love you so much and are so proud of you, and so am I. Our verses for VBS for the night were 1 John 4:9 and 2 Peter 3:18. They read: 1 John 4:9, 'This is how God showed his love among us: He sent his one and only Son into the world that we might live through him' (NIV). 2 Peter 3:18, 'But grow in the grace and knowledge of our LORD and Savior Jesus Christ. To him be glory both now and forever! Amen' (NIV)." She added, "I pray you grow in ways you never thought possible."

On Monday, she wrote, "You are in Louisville today, and I pray you are feeling all right. I still don't know where you slept, but I pray you are rested and fed. I wonder whom you have been able to talk to or what the church services were like that you went to. Have you eaten? Had a drink? I thank God for you and your passion for the lost. I pray that you get to minister to someone today." As I read that day, I realized that I was able to lead Samier, the hot dog vendor, to the LORD.

Tuesday, she wrote, "I miss you so much. I've prayed for you a lot today. I had a mini panic attack when the dramatic side in my head started playing a bunch of negative scenarios about your well-being. It took over me for a while, and finally I just asked God to give me peace. Shortly after that time, Miguel called me. He shared that a girl from Columbus, Ohio, had called in and said that you had helped her." I explained to my wife the situation that took place with Morgan. Apparently she had gotten to her friend's house okay, and she called my office and spoke to Miguel. It was that phone call that God used to give my wife peace.

While both of us sat on our couch with tears of joy and love, she wouldn't let go of my hand. She said, "Once I got that message, I was at complete peace. I didn't worry anymore and put my faith in God and trusted in Him, just like you were doing and what I was praying for you."

I was overwhelmed by God's touch on my wife and my family. She had grown so much, and I was so thankful, inspired, and proud of her. I said, "That was a city, a place, and a time that I wasn't even supposed to be in if I had stayed on my original plan." I was happy to hear that Morgan had arrived safely but was amazed by God's divine plan and how things transpired more than I knew. "I wonder what other things will take place because of this trip. I'm excited to know that one day all will be revealed, and I just pray that it continues to bring glory to God."

Everything else my wife wrote was without fear. If I stayed on my path and had been stubborn to do so, then I never would have met Morgan. Miguel never would have gotten her call, and Shannan wouldn't have received the message. She conveyed things that took place within her VBS class and more bowel movements from my sons, but her prayers changed from concern to praise.

She said, "My faith has grown from this experience. I know you are the one that left and took that first step of faith, but through this whole process, I grew as well." We prayed and thanked God for the life-changing experience that took place in our family's life over the past week. Now it was time to rest and share my stories with my family and friends the next day.

LIFE AFTER
THE JOURNEY

When I woke up, I had a completely changed mind-set of priorities. I didn't care what was taking place on ESPN but about seeing my son get ready for his day. Spending time with my family was the most pressing thing I had that morning. I had already spent time with the LORD while they slept, and He made it clear where the faith I had learned needed to be applied in my life. After spending time with my family, I went in to work. With tears of great joy, I shared how Jesus walked with me. A few of the people came up to me afterward and voiced how they could see a change.

I went to get in my car to run an errand when I noticed a young man in his early twenties walking down the street. I quickly got in my car and asked if I could give him a ride. He said, "Sure." My eyes had been opened to all the missed opportunities I'd had to love people. I took this time to share Jesus with him, and he was very interested in what I had to say. The week prior, I would have paid no attention to him and therefore would have missed the opportunity God had given me.

After taking him to the store, I ran my errand. On the way back I spotted the same young man walking down the street but without any groceries. I pulled over and found out he had left his money at home. I offered to drive him to his home and then back to the store, and he accepted. I invited him to be my guest at church on Sunday, and he said he would come with his grandmother. I offered to wait to give him a ride home, but he informed me that his grandmother was coming to get him. He allowed me to pray with him before leaving my car, and he said he was very grateful for the ride.

I drove back to the office thinking about how I could no longer allow the little things to pass me by. For my family and friends, it would take some time to see the full change in my life, but they all noticed that I was different. I continue to pray that I never lose what I gained on my faith walk. I keep hearing Billy in Chattanooga and the oldest brother in Columbus, who both said, "Be safe." I realized it isn't about being safe in what I am but *whose* I am. Daniel was kept safe in the lion's den because of his faith in God. Shadrach, Meshach, and Abednego, when told to worship the golden statue of King Nebuchadnezzar or they would be thrown into a blazing furnace, said this to the king:

> Shadrach, Meshach, and Abednego replied to
> him, "King Nebuchadnezzar, we do not need
> to defend ourselves before you in this matter.
> If we are thrown into the blazing furnace, the
> God we serve is able to deliver us from it, and
> he will deliver us from Your Majesty's hand.
> But even if he does not, we want you to know,

Your Majesty, that we will not serve your gods
or worship the image of gold you have set up."

Daniel 3:16–18 (NIV)

They were safe in whose they were. The fact they believed so purely in God that, even if God didn't spare them, they still wouldn't worship shows us how safe they were. I believe there are others that are willing to take a step of faith. I hope to get other church pew fillers out into the world for the cause of Christ.

Billy holding Naz. I met him in Chattanooga on my first day. Billy expressed his concern, compassion, and expression of love by giving me twenty dollars in order to make sure I would have something to eat.

This is Brath (behind the wheel) and Darrell from the church in Chattanooga. They gave me a lift to the shopping center where I would share Christ with the people present.

Daphnie, the kind woman who worked at the Greyhound station who bought me lunch and gave me ice for my knee.

Country Music Festival in Nashville with the ocean of people to talk to.

The Japanese congregation that embraced me and allowed me to take a shower in their rec center.

This is Amos, on his way back to Knoxville after attending his second wife's memorial service. Both of his wives had the same last name, Smith.

The beautiful Walnut Street church in Louisville, Kentucky.

The staff of Walnut Street church, who prayed over me and provided me with housing.

This is Raymond, whom I sat with on the city bench for over an hour while I was in Louisville. He became upset when I gave money to a man in need and then broke my heart when he said he actually wanted to go to hell so that "others could have a spot in heaven."

My hotel suite inside the Galt House.

My view from my room within the Galt House.

This is the young "evangelist" and his youth leader whose faith I had the opportunity to challenge while in the food court in Louisville.

This is Samier, the hot dog vendor in Louisville, who repented of his sins for the first time.

Me getting around in the rain wearing my poncho in Louisville.

This is the Muslim cab driver with whom I spoke for over an hour and half in an effort to explain to him that "Allah" and the "Living God" are not one and the same.

My first attempt to wash my clothes in a hotel bath and sink. (These were actually white when I left for my trip!)

This is Terry, the homeless man I met in Indianapolis. He asked, "How can I forgive my family for all the wrong they have done to me?

This is Patch, whom I met in Lexington. He actually said he loved being homeless. Here he is singing and playing his guitar after just having lunch with me and his friend Joe.

Me on the bus from Indianapolis to Columbus journaling my experience.

Me on the streets of Indianapolis.

FOR THE
READER

If you are not a Christian, please allow me to clearly share with you what it means to be one. The Bible says in Romans 3:23, "For all have sinned and fall short of the Glory of God" (NIV). Because of this, there is a consequence to our sin. His Word says in Romans 6:23, "For the wages of sin is death, but the gift of God is eternal life in Christ Jesus our LORD" (NIV). Everyone will die one day. Maybe you know someone close to you that has passed away. Unless you were to take your own life, you don't know when your last breath will be. There is a debt that has to be paid.

You may be thinking that you have done enough good things to get into heaven, that you are a good person. Well, His Scripture says, "We are all like an unclean thing, all of our righteousness are like filthy rags." According to Isaiah 64:6a (NIV), that means your parents, your local pastor, me, and you have all sinned against God. We are all lost. No deeds that we can do can pay our debt. But there is hope. Titus 3:5 (NIV) says, "Not by works of righteousness which we have done, but according to His mercy He saved us, through the washing of regeneration and renewing of the Holy Spirit." Ephesians 2:8–9 (NIV) says, "For by grace you have been saved, through faith, and not that of yourselves, it is the gift of God, not of works, lest anyone should boast."

The cost that is to be paid must come from someone that is sinless and blameless, One that is pure and holy. The only One who could ever be is God himself. So there is One that can pay the price, and better yet, He has already done that for you. Romans 5:8 (NIV) says, "But God demonstrates His own love toward us, in that while we're still sinners, Christ died for us." God wants you to be with Him in heaven. He doesn't want you to be apart from Him for one more moment. Romans 10:9–10 (NIV) says, "That if you confess with your mouth the LORD Jesus and believe in your heart that God has raised Him from the dead, you will be saved. For with the heart one believes unto righteousness, and with the mouth confession is made unto salvation."

So now, looking at what the Bible says on the reasons to be saved, this is how you can be: Tell God that you not only acknowledge that you have sinned against Him but that your judgment for that should be separation from Him for all eternity. In John 14:6 (NIV), Jesus said, "I am the way, the truth and the life, no one comes to the Father except through me." Believe that Jesus is God, that He was the only perfect and pure payment for your debt, and that He was crucified and died, was buried for three days, and arose again. He conquered death. His blood has washed you white as snow. From this day forth until you are with Him in heaven, you will turn from your sinful ways and put your faith in Christ. However you want to pray that prayer, He will meet you where you are at. I hope that you will join us in heaven one day, where He will be. Romans 10:13 (NIV) says, "For everyone who calls upon the LORD shall be saved."

For my brothers and sisters in Christ, thank you for taking the time to read my story. There are many other events and situations that took place that I didn't include in this book. Please don't think for a second that I did anything that couldn't be duplicated or replicated. For years, I sat in the church, gave my tithe, attended weekly, and even volunteered for extra church outings from time to time. However, when the time comes for me to be in heaven with my loving Savior, Jesus, I felt ashamed of what I would have said to Him. Maybe one of these applies to you: *Well, I gave you ten percent of what I earned; isn't that why you died? I worshiped in your house on Sundays and gave my time in the choir; isn't that why you sacrificed yourself for me? I was a pastor and preached your Word; isn't that enough?*

There are many books out there that are written by good, God-fearing people that will tell you what you need to do to live for Christ, but what you really need to do is stop attending church and *become* the church. Christ asked for our all, not for our version of a Christian routine. We are called to be in the world, not sitting in church. I'm not saying it isn't important to be a member of a congregation, but that cannot be what makes you a Christian. We are told to go out into the world and proclaim His name. In heaven, we will have the opportunity to give God gifts based off of how we lived our life for Christ. The reason why prayer was kicked out of school, abortion is allowed in some areas, and safer sex instead of abstinence is being taught is because we as Christians have stayed sitting in the church. How can we say that we are picking up our cross and following Jesus daily if daily we do nothing for Him? In the Gospel of John, in the fourteenth chapter Jesus says, "If you love me keep my commands." I desire to love Jesus more today than yesterday.

Wherever you are in your walk with the LORD, you can always go farther. Paul says in Philippians:

> Not that I have already obtained all this, or have already arrived at my goal, but I press on to take hold of that for which Christ Jesus took hold of me. Brothers and sisters, I do not consider myself yet to have taken hold of it. But one thing I do: Forgetting what is behind and straining toward what is ahead, I press on toward the goal to win the prize for which God has called me heavenward in Christ Jesus.
>
> Philippians 3:12–14 (NIV)

Paul himself never came to the place where he could do all that he could for Christ, so how could we ever think so? Just like I was given challenges out on my faith walk, here is one for you. Grab a pen and write it in this book. Make it so it cannot be erased and that you make it yours. Answer the following questions:

What do you believe?

_____

_____

_____

_____

Why do you believe it?

_____

_____

_____

_____

Do you trust God to provide everything for you?

_____

What have you done today that was specifically for Christ?

_____

_____

When is the last time you shared how Jesus changed your life?

_____

_____

When was the last time you helped someone you didn't know?

_____

_____

_____

If obeying Jesus shows Him our love, how much do you love Jesus?

_____

_____

_____

_____

Why are you willing to justify where you are now instead of choosing to grow more?

_____

_____

_____

Is fear the reason you will not move further in faith?

_____

_____

_____

_____

After reading this will you still choose to do nothing?

_____

We who believe in Christ as LORD and Savior are called to proclaim His name. It isn't a pastor's responsibility or a spiritual gift; it is a commandment. Though some are called for the purpose of profession, we are all supposed to not only live but share our faith. If you are ready to be bold and stand up against all that the world has against you, then pray. Pray for strength and courage to go beyond yourself and wisdom and patience for when you have the opportunity to interact with someone. Pray for boldness in the absence of support. Take a moment now and pray to God how you feel led. After prayer is done, start looking for opportunities to step out in faith and to test yourself in your faith. We cannot pick and choose what we will obey under God's commands and expect to bring Him glory. Full surrender with determined obedience is what is needed. Pastors, missionaries, and evangelists aren't the only ones responsible for sharing the great commission; we all are! When you see the first person that makes eye contact with you that you don't know, go tell them about Jesus. Pile high the treasures in heaven, for they are what you will give to Christ for the life you lived here on earth. I pray that they are mountains.

For encouragement and sharing with other faith walkers, visit www.survivingfaith.com. Godspeed!

e|LIVE

---

listen|imagine|view|experience

AUDIO BOOK DOWNLOAD INCLUDED WITH THIS BOOK!

In your hands you hold a complete digital entertainment package. In addition to the paper version, you receive a free download of the audio version of this book. Simply use the code listed below when visiting our website. Once downloaded to your computer, you can listen to the book through your computer's speakers, burn it to an audio CD or save the file to your portable music device (such as Apple's popular iPod) and listen on the go!

How to get your free audio book digital download:

1. Visit www.tatepublishing.com and click on the e|LIVE logo on the home page.
2. Enter the following coupon code:
   484d-095a-974b-1239-54a1-43d6-39e4-adeb
3. Download the audio book from your e|LIVE digital locker and begin enjoying your new digital entertainment package today!